P9-CBE-072

THE
WATERY
REALM

PETER GOW

"Meditation and water are wedded forever"
—Melville, *Moby-Dick*

WOODENBOAT BOOKS

Published by WoodenBoat Books
Naskeag Road, PO Box 78
Brooklin, Maine 04616 USA
www.woodenboat.com

ISBN–13: 978-0-937822-91-3
ISBN–10: 0-937922-91-4

Copyright 2006, Peter Gow

All rights reserved. No part of the contents of this
book may be reproduced in any form without written
consent of the publisher. All inquiries should be made
to WoodenBoat Books, PO Box 78, Brooklin, Maine
04616 USA.

BasRelief Design, Book Design
Heidi Gommo, Illustrator
Jane Crosen, Editor

Printed in China by Regent Publishing Services Ltd.

Library of Congress Cataloging-in-Publication Data
pending.
Gow, Peter, 1950–

First printing 2006
                10 9 8 7 6 5 4 3 2

CONTENTS

FOREWORD

The first time I encountered the sea I was a very small boy, and I have no memory of the occasion. Photographs of a family summer on the Peconic Bays of Long Island prove that it occurred, however. Whatever I may have learned that summer is lost in the mists of more than half a century's forgettings, denials, and conflations.

My true maritime education began in my own backyard in rural upstate New York, four hundred miles from salt water. My first sea was the creek that ran behind our house, broad enough to qualify as a river in New England and varied enough in its scapes to seem a miniature world—a bonsai ocean—to a child with a bucket, a butterfly net, and a developing understanding of the concept of patience.

In swimming holes, some created by manmade dams for reasons unknown and others carved from the gravelly bank of the floodplain, I discovered LIFE: fish, alive and visible to my eyes and swimming—just as my picturebooks showed—in beautiful, fluid schools. In the shallows, where I could wade onto the slippery rocks and reach into the water, crayfish darted under rocks, and my careful movements might be rewarded with an actual capture.

Along the bank small ponds had formed, seemingly cut off from any source, changing shape each year, but always present. Shaded by great willow trees, these little seas held life in superabundance, including frogs of several species, green newts and gorgeous red efts, waterbugs (that held no interest for me then or ever), and even turtles. In the spring gelatinous masses of frogs' eggs clung to waterlogged branches near the surface, and throughout the summer I could follow the transformation of sperm-like pollywogs into frogs, a process both marvelous and aesthetically absurd. In my eleventh summer, a biology teacher neighbor introduced me to the art of dissection, and several frogs yielded up to me the secrets of their anatomy against a backdrop of dark paraffin. It was an experiment I have never since cared to repeat.

At about the same time fate returned me to the vernal pleasures of the warm, sunny bays of the Eastern Seaboard. I discovered the joy of sailing a small boat by myself, and more recently I have taken up kayaking; but I am no expert at these and am certainly not driven to extreme, or even very strenuous or uncomfortable, performance. The vagaries of family and career have kept me on the Atlantic seaboard all of my adult life, and I have summered on salt water for more than half my years. In other years I have situated myself so as to be looking at or boating on bodies of fresh water of sufficient size to satisfy my craving for the sound of wind, waves, and seabirds—or loons.

My credentials as a world traveler are slim, but in my few journeys abroad I have continued to be drawn to the shore—of the Solent, of Lake Geneva, of the islands the Dodecanese, and of the Sea of Japan. My journeys in what Shelley called "realms of gold" have been wider, starting with the stories of Stevenson and Conrad and subsequently whole shelves full of books on whaling, sailing, undersea exploration, field guides (to all manner of creatures, plants, and landforms in, over, and around the sea), river-running, shipwrecks, and polar and South Seas adventures. As a sedentary, overweight, middle-aged father, I have lately developed an absolute, uncritical devotion to the novels of Patrick O'Brian. All this has inspired some bits of writing of my own, and there is clearly something essential and elemental in my fascination with all things wet.

Until lately I hadn't given my proclivity for the sea much thought as other than a personal quirk, but in my old age and at-last nascent self-awareness as an educator I have begun to wonder whether the learning experiences I have had in and about the waters of the Earth are not important in analogous ways to others. I wonder whether what I have learned from my exposure to things of the sea has not in some way been fundamental to my learning, to my sense of the world, and to my sense of myself as a competent (well, at least somewhat) grownup in the world.

As a society we seem to be setting aside, rather willingly, our sense of nature other than as a commodity, and American society (and American education) seems to be regarded as authentic and relevant only when it is urban. Others, from Aldo Leopold to Bill McKibben, have been decrying this trend for a century, and educational theorists from John Dewey onward have written eloquently of the need for experience, and especially experience of the natural world, in education. I do occasionally wonder whether the time may have passed when the sea has so much to teach us, or rather when we had the patience and inclination to learn from it.

It is not my intent here to condemn, nor do I wish to be a Jeremiah—or a spoilsport. This book came into being as I began to meditate on the meaning of the sea in my own learning and in my own thinking about teaching. In this extended meditation, it is my intent to offer up ideas and reflections on how it is that the human spirit, the learning spirit, seems to be so intimately connected with the waters of the world, large and small, and how those who teach, formally or informally, might call upon this connection to make our work perhaps easier, perhaps richer, perhaps more meaningful.

They do not know it, but my mother, Persis Gow; my uncle, Cyrus Collins; my spouse, Mimi Harrington; my brother, David Gow; and my dear friend Nat Philbrick—a mentor though a younger man—have together inspired this work. My mother first showed me the sea and then provided waterside accommodations for many of the happiest summers of my life. Uncle Cy taught me not only some of the techniques of sailing but also that sailing is not simply an activity but a way of being. A gifted teacher—of sailing and of other things—Mimi has made common sense of the business of teaching kids to sail and to regard themselves as sailors, part of a tradition of self-reliance and character; I hope that I have picked up a bit of the latter from her. David has transformed his early interest in the behavior of marine life into a life's work exploring and teaching about the boundaries between the brain, consciousness, and culture, a vocation that seems very much of a piece with his year-round sea-kayaking on the New England coast and skinny-dipping at his family's summer place in New Hampshire. Nat simply had the nerve to teach me to write, undoing twenty years of schooling and releasing me to explore my own thinking on many subjects in new ways; it hasn't hurt that he also is a brilliant sailor and an even more brilliant historian of the sea and maritime society. To these five I give my thanks, and to them I dedicate this work.

A note on content. Specific references in this book are based on what I know, what I have learned, or what I remember and most emphatically not on "research." Were this book intended to be a compendium of resources, it would be different in tone and in the level of detail.

I allude to places, to books, to historical events as archetypes, as models, as examples only. My vintage and heritage alike have perhaps limited my frame of reference to the Western and even more to the American. For those who might dismiss this work as being insufficiently multicultural, I can offer my apologies and an earnest pledge to keep learning, as I have been learning all along from colleagues and friends, in the word and in the flesh.

More importantly, I believe that there will always be children standing on a beach or at the end of a pier, transfixed by the sight of the passing boats or a flight of shore birds. In the late afternoon, after the lifeguards have gone off duty and the fishermen have returned to their homes, a handful of kids will come to swim in the waves or skip pebbles across water. One grandchild out of a half-dozen will catch the fishing bug and pump the old-timers for all their lore. A few youngsters will return to their camps or clubs to hone their skills as sailors or canoeists. The call of the sea—a wild call and a clear call, as John Masefield reminds us—is with us always, if we would but listen.

Peter Gow
Essex, New York

I. Ocean

An ocean is where you find it. As a child I was puzzled by the term "Seven Seas"; anyone looking at a map can see that there are many more than that. Furthermore, my National Geographic globe, with its plastic skullcap, indicated that seas were part of oceans, but that oceans met oceans in some way that seemed to lack the clearly colored demarcations that separated nations and even continents.

The child whose attention is drawn to maps and globes and who can be inveigled into making a study of their content—in the best of all worlds not by the demands of a school curriculum but by a household or a friendship that places value on building an awareness of these things—has a great gift. The thousand-dollar illuminated globe on its library stand is not required; a tattered road map will suffice. The child susceptible to cartographic temptation learns not only about scale, about the smallness of one's own existence on the vastness of the Earth, but also about possibility: of a whole world to see, of places, defined by nature and developed and named by our own species, to dream of, to go to, and to protect. The child cradling a globe holds, in a figurative sense, the world, a sacred trust that can be dimly understood by any child old enough to understand the concept of representation.

The globe is covered with oceans, or rather with ocean—a single, connected expanse comprising a vast blue field onto which landmasses are set, like floating islands; ocean is the default, land is the exception. The connectedness mystifies and compels; a child's finger can trace a path from the Atlantic Ocean through the English Channel into the North Sea and thence to the Baltic, unknowingly recapitulating some of the world's great trade routes and the rise of the city-states of the Hansa. Where does one body of water begin and another end? Mariners, it seems, know this—the boundaries set by custom and by geographic feature—but a child with a map must take it on faith that such boundaries exist. But the child may also surmise that such boundaries do not much matter.

The child fascinated by the compact, highly decorated orb of a good globe or whose eye naturally focuses toward the finest level of detail on a global or continental map is introduced to a world of infinite seas. Subdividing the greatness of "ocean" and covering landmasses with cheerful blue dots of many kinds, the seemingly infinite seas—including lakes of all sizes down to ponds and "land" in its soggier forms; swamps and bogs, for example—add to the notion of a world indeed defined by water.

The child looking at the broad unbroken bands of blue on a globe knows that something more important than the convention of names is going on. The surface of the globe, the child knows, is a model of something more wild, more unbounded, more fundamental; for something so huge, the little black letters account for little, at least much beyond the three labels placed on the "true" oceans in their encirclement of the Earth: Atlantic,

Pacific, and Indian. The rest is just detail.

But the details can be profoundly interesting. The child soon learns, from school, from the conversations of adults, that the Mediterranean Sea (not an ocean, even) is substantially more important than its size might warrant. The Caribbean is the same. What makes this so? The Mediterranean encompasses Egypt and Greece and Italy, the three ancient civilizations the child is likely to encounter first in social studies classes as the "horizon" of knowledge expands beyond home, town, state, and nation. The Caribbean received the dubious bounty of Europe's first attentions upon the "discovery" of the Americas.

But there are full-fledged oceans that don't seem to matter. The Arctic and Antarctic are cold and remote— even the child can see that. Since the International Geophysical Year of 1957–58, there has been little that might draw the attention of a child to the polar seas, except perhaps recent "expeditions"—often groups of enthusiasts of extreme sports—that create interactive websites using satellite links in order to entice school classes to follow their progress across frozen wastes and thus to entice sponsors to support the "educational" purposes of their adventure. But the oceans, ice-clogged and distant, play a relatively small role in the learning such enterprises engender. Some seas, like the Caspian, the China, and the Arabian, seem at first glance to be of importance disproportionate to their size. The latter two take their names from the lands they touch, inverting the case of the Atlantic Seaboard or the Pacific Coast, dominated by and named for the sea that touches them.

The relationship of seas and lakes with moving water also invites speculation. A dam compresses a river into the blue splotch of a lake, which suddenly narrows again into a thin black line. Rivers broaden without manmade obstruction into their own thin blue streaks. The energetic flow of virtually all rivers dissipates into the calm breadth of an ocean, sea, or lake, sometimes with the added drama of a delta and sometimes just of a sudden; how does the geographer decide where the Amazon, for example, ends and the Atlantic begins? Sometimes the river seems to become something else, like the grass floes of Nile's Sudd, before rediscovering its riverine purpose and pushing on, at last debouching into still water.

Time takes on a different meaning when we look at maps of water. The river suggests its distance in time; describing a river's route requires words like next, and then, or after—the notation of a future unfolding in space. Two centuries ago the *Bounty* mutineers protected themselves for decades by settling an island of surpassing remoteness. Just one century ago, the time it might take to steam from New York to Liverpool or from Southampton to Calcutta still mattered. Tahiti and Australia were unimaginably far away, the swath of blueness dividing them from Europe or America or even Africa as wide as the eyes of a traveler contemplating a journey to those parts. Jet travel has, in the cliché, shrunk the globe, but the distance to a destination away from the main air routes can still sometimes be measured in days, not hours. To familiarize oneself with a map is to begin to see the world in terms of time as well as space. The world may shrink, but the fundamental unit of measure for humans is time—a finite personal resource in an infinite universe. In a world when few bother to travel great distances on water, preferring to be over it, the great gaps between land must still be noted, accommodated for. The world is large, and the sea, reminding us by its vastness of the premium we must place on time, defines its largeness in four dimensions.

Perhaps the most startling views of the sea are

those that turn the waters themselves invisible and present the user merely with a view of so many bottoms, pieced together from hydrographic observations. With their vital fluid removed, oceans, seas, and lakes are as if stripped naked, their mysteries revealed. The greatest of oceans seem a bit paltry, with features too few or too regular to be of much interest—a view confirmed by photographs returned from the sites of deep-ocean shipwrecks, with the blue-gray ghosts of great liners and battlewagons in silty relief against an otherwise barren blue-gray bottom; where are the mermaids, treasure chests, and waving fronds of seaweed we were taught to expect in Davy Jones' locker? The hypnotically regular striations of tectonic rift patterns or soaring mountains—Hawaii rising higher than Everest—cannot quite make up for the sterility of those empty basins. The human eye seeks complexity, but somehow it would rather see an endless surface of waves than a god's-eye view of the oceans, drained.

When we look at a map we see the ocean in our mind's eye, fluid, heaving, teeming with life. But we are touched even more deeply when we have occasion to fly over water, living out what for many is a recurring dream. High over the middle of the ocean on a clear day, we can even see the curvature of the Earth, personal affirmation that Columbus was right, and we delight in the infinite sparkle of moving waves or—better still—the path of light that moves along the water to connect our vantage point with the sun or moon when they are low in the sky. In places fractalized coastlines mark the land's margins—the bays, islands, and coves of northern New England and the Northwest—and in others there are vast expanses of yellow beach with parallel chalklines of surf. We ache to reach down and trail our fingers along where the surfaces meet, the cool water and the rough, plastic ground. Over rivers and lakes sudden quicksilver squiggles or coin-bright ovoids change to brown, green, or—most rarely and most wonderfully—blue as we pass over; occasionally the waters are so clear or so filled with vegetation that we cannot tell where the water ends and the land begins. All this is beauty, confirming what the map has told. With our foreheads pressed against the scratched Perspex of an airplane window, we see the representation become the reality.

In the imagination of the child whose attention has been brought to the world of maps, and then to the world itself, the idea takes form that the Earth is indeed a place of infinite variety and infinite interest. The wonders of nature are many, and the sea brings those wonders literally into relief, but wonders also lie where land and water converge and where humankind must confront and engage with an environment to which we are not ourselves by nature suited.

II. FRONTIER

Humanity's first frontier was water. The technique required to climb the highest mountain or to cross the widest desert is little different from that needed to cross a room: put one foot ahead of the other; repeat. The hazards of altitude, cold, or dehydration will manifest themselves, but covering ground is largely a matter of logistics, and will.

Crossing water is fundamentally different. Whether or not our ancestors dragged themselves out of the sea, the human body instinctively hesitates before entering water, where depth, or current, or cold, or beasts may revoke the gift of life. "Unfamiliar waters," in the literal as well as metaphorical sense, denotes risk and invokes the need for caution. A river's edge or a shore facing open water are the simplest and most familiar of frontiers.

Perhaps the ease with which we have brought the waters of the world under our control, or the speed with which we have distanced ourselves from an essential vocational relationship with the sea, has made us forget the nature of the many aqueous frontiers that challenged our ancestors. The diesel ferry that slides us from mainland to island without even requiring us to leave our automobiles, the frost-covered bags of Indonesian shrimp in the grocer's freezer, the parade of European sport sedans whistling past us on the interstate, the spans of bridges that lift us across streams, rivers, and bays—none of these requires us to consider, even for a moment, the height of the water, the state of the tide, or the weather forecast. The waters have been tamed. If we choose to embark upon them for recreation, that is our lookout, our choice.

Not so long ago, however, that ferry route might have been a treacherous passage for a sail—or oar-driven craft—a run from Scylla to Charybdis. A Discovery Channel documentary on shrimp might include sobering shots of Southeast Asian fishermen in small boats gathering their catch in frightening conditions, and North Atlantic hurricanes might well have diverted the great container ship full of sleek gray coupes from its intended course as the ship's officers nervously monitored weather transmissions and argued with land-bound company bureaucrats concerned that the slightest deviation meant more fuel burned, less profit made. The largest of bridges almost all have somewhere at the base of their structures small plaques commemorating those who died in their construction: high steel and water are a deadly combination, pitting lifelines and rigging against wind, exhaustion, and gravity; one hand for the work, one hand for yourself remains the rule.

Children first learn of water's frontier nature from their own experience. Spend a few hours on a beach or at poolside, watching small children in their first encounters with water. In their tentative steps, their squeals of terror and delight, and their desperate grasp on parents or floating toys, they recapitulate all of human history with water. In time, they "master" the element—with swimming strokes, with flotation devices, and in time perhaps in small boats—but in truth they have mastered only a selected segment, carefully chosen for size, temperature, placidity, and cleanliness. Even the most competent children realize this, as can be witnessed in their wide stares and fluttering stomachs as the family car climbs the rise of a great bridge; the parent at the wheel may be thinking only of the tollbooth ahead, but the children are viscerally aware of something else. A life jacket, or being able to swim, is not always enough.

In our society's past, the sea was as legitimate a destination for the young person seeking to make his or her fortune as the West. For the Pilgrims and the millions of less exalted emigrants who set sail from Europe to the Americas, the sea was the ultimate frontier, and demographic history suggests that it was enough for many—the seaboards and their cities filled quickly and have remained more densely populated than the hinterland. The occupants of the narrow margins of soil occupied by the Thirteen Colonies were for the most part looking toward the sea more often than across the mountains; the dependence of the colonists on European trade goods made the penetration of the westward territories more of a novelty or an occasional cruel necessity than a typical activity. Young men in Boston, New York, and Charleston dreamed of running away to sea, and not because the life of a sailor was easier than the life of a backwoodsman. Native Americans carried tomahawks, but South Sea islanders were reputed to be cannibals; no woodland cabins were ever sunk with all hands in a blizzard in plain view of stupefied, helpless neighbors, a common occurrence when a coastal ship ran too close to shore in a winter storm. Settlers on the woodland frontier may have been hungry and cold, but they dwelt in relative security compared to those who went down to the sea in ships.

For North America the maritime imperative was intensified by the potential for wealth that lay in such coastal resources as fish and whales. Americans could scarcely not have gone down to the sea in ships, considering the chances for making a good living that swam beneath the surface. While a handful of mountain men "tamed the wilderness" by learning survival skills in quest of dead rodent skins in the ranges and forests of the trans-Appalachian and then trans-Mississippi west, many thousands of their neighbors became expert mariners, mining the seas for fishy fortunes and piling up riches by shuttling goods around the Atlantic world. Improvements and rationalizations in navigation, commercial finance, and ship design helped tame a grander and, it must be admitted, more significant frontier. Frémont conquered California, but until the transcontinental railroad was completed the most efficient way to get there was by sea, around Cape Horn on a voyage so epic that mariners who repeat it even in our own time are held in awe. While the Pathfinder and his band of soldiers wandered the Southwest, his naval counterpart, Charles Wilkes, traversed half the globe in the name of his country.

Before James Fenimore Cooper brought forth *The Deerslayer*, he had already earned fame as the author of longwinded potboilers of the sea. *The Red Rover*, *The Pilot*, and *The Water-Witch* are among the first sea stories, and the virtues of their eponymous protagonists—plain-spokenness bordering on the blistering, true-heartedness (even when behaving in a way that was technically criminal), and a mind-boggling mastery of the technical skills of seamanship and naval warfare—were only later echoed in the skillset shared by Natty Bumppo and his Mohican companions. Scholars have speculated that there is something in the dark mysteries of the forest and its denizens that tickles the troubled spirit of The American—hence the reputational triumph of Hawkeye over the Skimmer of the Seas— but the American sea story has had a proud tradition, from Herman Melville to Jack London all the way down to Jimmy Buffett.

In the twentieth century, maritime nonfiction began to trump fiction, perhaps owing to the dreadful representation of the unsinkable *Titanic* sliding beneath cold, glassy seas as the world looked on, again helpless. The manifold horrors of war at sea turned out to be much worse in the absence of pine tar and canvas—the sinking of the *Lusitania* in view of the Irish coast, HMS *Hood* obliterated, the spectacle of Pearl Harbor in newsreels endlessly replayed. Many a thousand gone, in moments.

In a more benign realm, poets and novelists have posted their own pickets on the watery frontiers of the soul. The emotional gulfs in human experience are made manifest in the East River of Whitman's "Crossing Brooklyn Ferry" and Hart Crane's "The Bridge" and even more poignantly on the beach of Whitman's primordial revelation in "Out of the Cradle, Endlessly Rocking." The Congo and Thames serve Joseph Conrad as parallel paths into the *Heart of Darkness*, and Conrad joins his forebears Defoe and Swift in giving protagonists stormy seas to endure in "night journeys" to the other side of human nature; Lord Jim finds darkness where Robinson Crusoe finds strength and Lemuel Gulliver finds absurdity. In more ancient literatures, Gilgamesh and Odysseus encounter turbulent seas in their own ways, and the fishermen-disciples of Jesus, it might be remembered, find faith in a storm. The list goes on.

It has been left to a handful of adventurers, some of them perhaps half-crazed in their deliberate zeal, to remind us periodically that the sea remains a frontier. Sometimes it involves a thoroughly ridiculous "world record" voyage—across the ocean in a boat the size of a bathtub, a singlehanded circumnavigation by a septuagenarian or teenager. Less exciting to the tabloids but no less fraught with danger and dark possibility are more purposeful assaults on the ocean's extremes, such as the deep-sea exploration of historic wrecks or the quest for understanding of new deep-ocean life forms or geological wonders.

Sometimes the motivations behind these adventures are all too familiar. We read of professional sailors, not so much "yachtsmen" as durable assemblages of muscle, skill, and experience perennially available to crew "extreme" ocean races popular with European fans. These heroes (for so we must regard them) seem to be simply too acclimated to life under the intense conditions of high seas and high winds that characterize such races (most of the racing takes place in the "Southern Ocean"— the unbroken expanse of cold, fast-flowing sea south of 40° south latitude) to even conceive of coming ashore. Confirmed salts in the Age of Sail were even said to have been married to the sea. The adrenalin rush and the sheer feeling of competence in the never-ending test of a harsh environment are addictive nowadays just as they once were when that environment was visibly essential to everyone.

For landsmen who feel the urge to "take on" the watery frontier, ways to do so abound. There are "windjammer" cruises aboard authentic wooden schooners or sea-kayak treks among remote island chains. A good blow can turn any of these into a true test of skill and, survivors would argue, character. Children learn to canoe, sail, and windsurf at camps and clubs and in recreation programs, and the rite of passage in this type of education invariably involves either a solo venture or recovery from some imposed catastrophe—often both. The spirit of the frontiersman, according to our national mythology, lives within us, and the ability to confront and survive a challenge on the water has been sanctified as a way to prove it.

For the small child setting out in a pram on a first sail alone or for the leathery oceanographer planning to take a submersible into the Challenger Deep; for the hiker faced with a mountain stream of uncertain depth or the professional sailor signing on for yet another global trimaran race, the waters of the Earth remain a frontier, and the human spirit remains buoyantly eager to conquer it.

WR

III. FISH

Although People for the Ethical Treatment of Animals would violently disagree, the slogan "A bad day fishing is better than a good day working" resonates deeply within the experience of many people. Whether one is harvesting the waters vocationally or as a casual hobby, fishing is, perhaps because of the immutable wildness of the quarry and the arduous, almost impossible conditions in which it is often carried out, both mortally rewarding and mortally demanding; fishing provides, but it also demands. To fish is to partake in one of humanity's oldest and most, well, human activities.

Not a small part of the power of fishing in its varieties has been the opportunity offered to pass knowledge—deep knowledge, and deep wisdom—to rising generations. Children learn to fish with parents or grandparents and then, as parents or grandparents themselves, pass on the technique. Sometimes this is as simple as baiting a hook, while in other circumstances the act of catching a fish becomes the embodiment of an entire culture.

I come from a non-fishing family—my paternal relatives don't even seem to eat fish in any form—and so my own understanding of the art and place of angling has been slow to form and probably stunted. But I know well that my very first awareness of my own role in the cycle of life and death came when a cousin demonstrated to me how to slide an earthworm—even the name is terrestrial—onto a barbed hook, to be cast into the water in hopes of catching whatever swam there. I was killing, or at least mortally wounding, a living creature in an effort to catch—and kill—yet another one. I had never heard of a food chain, but I was now a part of it, even more irrevocably than when I had eaten my first spoonfuls of ground meat from a baby food jar or my first Fourth of July hot dog. To eat was to kill. And so it remains, until as a species we evolve to a more circumspect plane on which our view of what is edible ceases to include what is sentient, or at least what respires.

The steps of fishing are a ritual: bait-gathering; preparation of lines, nets, or traps; the journey to the fishing grounds; the casting of the apparatus upon the waters; the retrieval, with catch; and the preparation of the product ("cleaning," we say, as if the creature that has lived its life in water is somehow dirty, whereas "gutting" is a word more vigorous and more anatomically correct). Each step requires the fisherman to exercise age-old skills in age-old ways that the young accomplice will learn in turn.

And then there is the catch itself. Fish are sleek and beautiful in ways that have bewitched mankind from ancient times, instantly responsive to their environment and unimaginably swift: streamlined arrows of muscle and grace unmatched by human design until the first metal-skinned aircraft of the twentieth century, although some of the great designers of clippers and yachts a hundred years previous had tried with some success to capture the form. Fish carry exuberant, descriptive, even onomato-poetic names—barracuda, sunfish, tautog, mahi-mahi—and swarm the reefs and shallow reaches of the world.

They even fly, an act so unlikely that tales of starving mariners saved by flying fish landing on a parched deck are so implausible as to seem biblical. And beyond our knowledge, deep in the darkest reaches of the sea, lie exotic monsters glimpsed for but a moment in the floodlights of descending explorers or hauled, their bodies exploding in the low pressure of the surface, from the depths to the wonderment and perhaps terror of surprised fishermen. Rumors of monsters (There be dragons!) continue to titillate and frighten us, whether they relate to the fancied—the Loch Ness Monster or "Champy" in Lake Champlain—or to preternatural reality of the Great White Shark, which truly does appear on occasion to be suddenly inspired to cruise resort beaches in search of human flesh. Even as we munch our tuna melts, we do not regard this turnabout as fair play.

Since the time of Jonah, early victim of a man-eating sea creature, whales have been called fish. Even Melville, pressed for a plot summary of *Moby-Dick*, is reputed to have said, "It's about this fish." In the important but obscure novel, *Miriam Coffin*, or *The Whale-Fishers*, Joseph C. Hart recounts the ways in which Nantucketers in the peak years of the whaling industry went a-fishing. It's significant that in those years a young man of the island stood little chance of attracting the most desirable girls until he had harpooned a whale, and a bit of extra hazard or derring-do in the killing favored the lad even more in the island's human game of natural selection. These greatest of "fish" have been transformed in popular culture of late into human cousins, and even the dullest elementary-school student knows that whales are not fish but rather mammals with brains the size of watermelons who can sing weird songs that their teachers call beautiful. Endangered and anthropomorphic "gentle giants of the sea," whales and all their pelagic mammalian kin from seals to dolphins are the perfect politically correct subject for school study, where the child who can differentiate the baleen from the toothed and the pinniped from the cetacean has been baptized in guilt and awe. The study of whales even provides its own ironies and complexities: What is the student to think about traditional Arctic peoples who insist on hunting whales from motorboats as part of their cultural heritage, or what must one think of the orca— truly an eating machine—or the adorable seals that gobble up still cuter and more Disneyesque penguins and puffins?

Even those sea creatures that do not make the lists of cutest or most hydrodynamic please us. The flesh of the hideous lobster, shrimp, and crab yields up a succulence that excuses ugliness, and the edible bivalves— mussels, clams, scallops, and the like—tempt us with flavor and promises: of strength of character, like the indigenous peoples whose shell mounds can be found on any shore, or of sexual prowess, as embodied in the unlikely oyster.

(It is also interesting to note that, among all the animals killed and eaten by humans, only seafood is so often eaten or served whole or raw. We slurp oysters using their own shells as dishes and crunch oily sardines whole from their crowded can. Crabs and lobsters are dropped alive into kettles of boiling water and presented, steaming and whole, to avid diners along with specialized tools for extracting the edible parts from their calciferous casings. Not even the most complete of English meat pies includes so much of the land mammals whose innards they contain. Nowhere else—except perhaps for "gross-outs" involving bugs—does the child experience with such immediacy the visceral actuality of eating from the animal kingdom.)

The child who is invited to accompany elders on a fishing trip or just for a walk out on the flats to rake clams is thus invited into a world rich in meaning. Like the young Manolin of Hemingway's *The Old Man and the Sea*, the apprentice fisherman or clamdigger will learn the need for patience in locating the catch and perseverance, even stoicism, in the face of discomfort and perhaps danger. Each year's summer newspapers tell of multigenerational groups swept away while fishing, turning the outing in the family motorboat into something worse than the last voyage of the *Pequod*; Ishmael, at least, was left to tell thee. But we will not dwell on this aspect of fishing here.

We shall speak elsewhere about the virtues of seamanship, boathandling, knot-craft, and weather-reading as essential and valuable skills for the learning mariner and for all children; and that all these skills are (as it were) incidental to the business of fishing makes them no less important. Along the way the youngster going fishing may also learn to row a boat, balance a canoe, or safely stow a mess of gear—actions requiring care, attention, and common sense. A bit of carelessness in any of these tasks can have dire, or at least damp, consequences, providing a secondary lesson that adds to the significance of the experience.

The child learning to fish must, as I once did, confront the reality of the baited hook, and if luck is with the young angler, the more perplexing reality of a frightened, living fish, its jaw bleeding from the puncture wound, that must be taken off the hook and either replaced in its element or stunned into accepting its place in the death-chamber of creel or cooler. The landing of a fish, more perhaps than actually hooking it, is for the novice the most intense moment of the expedition. There is even the possibility that the fish might choose to bite back, a real worry when a toothy species is on the line or when the prey has pincers. But here the youngster must find the steel to do what is necessary, for also awakened is a sudden awareness that the suffering of the fish is a cruelty consciously inflicted. It must be ended quickly in the name of mercy as well as practicality.

For some species the game is in the fisherman's ability to "play" the fish, certainly an inapposite term from the fish's point of view. Ernest Hemingway famously defined the macho image of the deep-sea fisherman, tanned, hardened, with eyes always searching the middle distance for signs of fish, the great pole rising from his crotch in a symbolism so embarrassingly obvious it might make one wonder why anyone would willingly enact it. This fisherman is beautifully caricatured in the shark-obsessed Quint in *Jaws*, the novel (written by a sometime Nantucketer) and the film—a sea-hunter rendered so mad by his experience with sharks in World War II as to make Captain Ahab's consideration of the White Whale look positively measured. These are the extremes the deep-sea fisherman can reach, cautionary tales for the child hauling in his first bass or bluefish against an auditory backdrop of adult encouragement—"Not so fast! Easy! Easy!"—and the whine and ratchet-click of the reel. The wise child—and the wiser mentor—looks for better lessons in the patience of Hemingway's Santiago, for whom "the great fish," found and lost, is a phantasmagoria, like the dream of the lions. The circumspect fisherman concludes that in the end the fish will come willy-nilly; volition is in the fish, and the fisher can bring only patience to the game.

Recently a new sort of obsession has grown around the ancient and honorable sport of dry-fly fishing, now as equipment- and destination-fixated an activity for the affluent as the creation of the perfect stereo system was a couple of decades ago. Along with an arcana of gadgets, from split-bamboo rods to an infinitude of flies themselves, there is also the allure of place associated with fly-fishing in ways that transcend even the equation Maine-equals-lobster. Hidden pools in the narrowest branches of inaccessible rivers in remote locales offer, if not always great fish, a raconteur's dream of a travel tale well-told, with the potential for mouth-watering landscape description thrown into the bargain. If the quarry is oceanic, then the fly-fisherman goes flats-fishing in some tropical paradise, hoping to catch a trophy of a fish on a laughably light bit of tackle—the realization of another manly dream of physical compensation. For those who truly embrace the sport and not simply its trappings, the heart lies in twin requirements. The first is the iron discipline of a technique that is unchanged over centuries and that must be taught, preferably by a master, in order to be learned. The second is an empathy with fish, a kenning that transforms tying and casting the fly into a loving, personal, and sacred thank-offering in anticipation of the rise and strike of the fish.

Fly-fishing also distills the essentialness of place that marks all kinds of fishing. To know a stream, a pond, a lake, or a bay as a good fisherman knows it is to inhabit a nexus of factors from meteorology to geology, to know the "ground" below, and above all to know how the interplay of tide, current, and light affect the behavior of both the quarry fish and their natural prey—a subject in which the fish being sought are themselves necessarily experts.

For the committed fly-fisherman, this deep engagement with fish is only a more cultivated version of an awareness of the balance between man and creature shared by all who fish well or seriously. This awareness is no less present in the New England lobsterman or the Chesapeake Bay sailor dredging for oysters. The crew of the Grand Banks schooner *We're Here* in Kipling's *Captains Courageous* is packed with men who feel a bond not only with the sea but with the cod beneath it; Captain

Disko Troop is held in awe by the entire fishing fleet for his ability to think like a fish—to be "in fact, for an hour a cod himself."

The literature of fishing is filled with coming-of-age stories. Writers from Kipling to Hemingway to Norman Maclean have built their reputations on works in which the young are taught the great lessons of life through fishing, along the way evoking land- and seascapes of extraordinary power and beauty; who has not wanted to fish the Big Two-Hearted River of the mind? But *Captains Courageous* sets the standard, as few literary characters are as transformed as young Harvey Cheyne, the rotten child of a millionaire who becomes a four-square young man during his months aboard the *We're Here*. Harvey's experiences include witnessing death and madness close-up as well as being himself redeemed by brutal physical labor—the fundamental factor that set the life of the working man of the Industrial Revolution apart from that of Gilded Age grandees like Harvey and his father (who had, it turns out, built the first part of his fortune by the sweat of his brow). The Christ-like fisherman Manuel reminds the reader that fishing as a profession has long been associated with probity and honor. (This association is notably absent from today's stereotype of the recreational fisherman, branded as being ever-ready to lie about The One That Got Away.)

Even if we are ourselves alienated from the act of fishing, we are none of us alienated from fish and from the metaphorical prevalence of fishing. If we do not choose to eat seafood, we know about it, and we know about it well, simply by virtue of our residence on a watery planet. We teach a child to fish not so much that they might eat as that they might live a life that is somehow connected in the most basic ways to the sea.

IV. Language

Nonsailors invited to spend time aboard a boat are often put off by the insistence of even the most casual "yachtsman" on using the technical language of the sea. This seems confusing, pretentious, fussy. Why not call the front the front, the left the left? Those who spend time afloat and who have been mentored in seamanship or boatkeeping may have hundreds of words to describe what the landsman sees only as "that rope to pull up the sail" or the toilet.

Seagoing language is as much a part of our experience of oceans, lakes, and rivers as the very sight of the water itself. Aboard vessels, large and small, terminology has evolved over the centuries for reasons that touch the existential anxieties of sailors. Even on land, we use a rich vocabulary to describe the shape and features of the littoral upon which we dwell. The child growing up on and around water needs to master the argot of sailing and navigation not simply to sound "salty" or to pass the state online boat-driving test, but rather for reasons of life and death.

No one doubts for a moment that pilots and air-traffic controllers need to have a shared vocabulary, intensely technical and detailed. A message misunderstood would be, we see, fatal. For the weekend sailor chatting easily with a friend aboard a small sailboat as they cross a lake or small bay on a Sunday afternoon, the urgency of air-traffic is a distant thought, but yet, as the skipper carries out even the most fundamental maneuvers, the choreography of movement required is designed to avoid catastrophe—the passenger being clunked in the head with the boom, a line caught on an arm or foot, a dunking, and perhaps the need for rescue. The proper choreography is accomplished through language, often pre-explained and rehearsed, that alerts the landsman to what is about to occur and where potential problems lie.

In less placid circumstances the precision of maritime language, the thousand terms for pieces, lines, directions, and conditions, saves not just inconvenience but lives. The sometimes harsh, unforgiving tutelage under which apprentice seamen, from impressed sailors in Nelson's British navy to willing cadets on modern sail-training ships or even in the merchant marine, "learn the ropes" of a ship—line by line, part by part—is designed to allow these men and women to respond reflexively and accurately to the commands that will enable the ship to survive extreme circumstances and maneuver in confined spaces—and to do this with a minimum of error, danger, and fuss. More than in most other situations, words matter at sea.

Dictionaries have been written cataloguing the intoxicating variety of maritime terminology. From charley nobles to mizzen chains, from top-gallants to gudgeons, the pieces of a ship represent a nomenclatural cornucopia, and there is great satisfaction to be gained from mastering the basics—bow and stern, port and starboard, halyard and sheet—and then moving on to the more esoteric, including the most obscure structural components of a boat or ship or the full complement of a clipper ship's sails and lines. The young person who can board an exhibited "tall ship" or historic vessel and name a few of the parts with confidence will have a satisfying sense of mastery, and if that same person can claim linguistic competence in a boat underway, regardless of its size or type or mode of power, practical competence will almost automatically follow. At sea, learning what is a prerequisite to learning how. The deeper one digs into the mountain of words related to ships and the sea, the more one understands about how things are done, and done correctly, in a way that inducts one into a separate world of experience and technique. We love the language of Long John Silver in Stevenson's *Treasure Island*, and for all that we detest Silver's actions, we are intensely jealous of the knowledge that he bestows upon Jim Hawkins; the squire and doctor may be moral exemplars, but Silver initiates Jim into the true mysteries of the sea, and his language—the medium—is much of the message.

The language of the sea has a taxonomic beauty— a multitude of categories, each containing its own subcategories. The landsman's generalized class of "knots" breaks into knots and bends and hitches, each coming in many varieties and each variety with its special virtues and uses; the rolling hitch can do what the clove hitch will not, the sheet bend holds where the anchor bend might fail. And then the whole category explodes into a world of fancy ropework that is specialized not so much by suitability as by aesthetic qualities. (This fancywork, like the carved whale-teeth known as scrimshaw, is largely a tribute not just to the innate creativity of sailors but often to the sheer boredom they experienced.)

The youngster looking at a nautical chart—proper terminology for a map designed to be used for navigation— will note a similar panoply of terminology reserved for mariners. Features of the coastline, bays, harbors, and coves, give way in some of the less-traveled places to guts, holes, and reaches. Interestingly, these terms have held on in places as picturesque as the words themselves. One doesn't enter New York Harbor through a reach (although one must pass a sandy hook) but one does enter some of the prime cruising grounds of New England through Eggemoggin Reach, Quick's Hole, and Plum Gut. When wind-powered, small-time shipping was the essence of the coastal economy, a skipper's ability to sail through a narrow passage with a minimum of maneuvering or to cut as close as possible to rocks, ledges, and reefs (perhaps unmarked and present in the minds only of those with "local knowledge") could earn a premium, and perhaps the crude precision of the place-names themselves warned competitors away. In all events, coastal charts are replete with a delicious variety of colorfully named locales, and even where these are lacking, the fine print—"Wreck Reported," "WARNING: Cable Crossing," "Shoal"—tells its own tale of history and danger.

Treacherous features may have been named by frightened or frustrated navigators at their most sardonic, but in the same vein there is a sometimes laughable sameness to place names, reflecting the limits to language and imagination that our ancestors must have reached fairly quickly as they encountered a world where all to be seen was new. The plethora of Long Islands, Long Lakes, and Long Ponds, of Stony Points and Cedar Islands, of Bear Islands and North Havens, gives a hint of a time when enough was enough and when semiliterate settlers just wanted to find a place of surcease from their restless movement. One craves the singularity of those Indian names that have survived. The tantalizing gumbo of Indian place names on Gulf Coast of Louisiana, Mississippi, Alabama, and Florida—from Pascagoula to Tallahassee, long the home waters of skilled indigenous navigators—is a meaningful mouthful of syllables and historical allusion, though to a history now largely gone with the wind.

Coastal and riverine place names in the United States tell the story of conquest and genocide as succinctly. Follow the Mississippi watershed from Eau Claire past St. Louis to New Orleans, and see the imperial wall built by French fur-traders and Jesuits to surround the Thirteen Colonies of the British. Trail your fingers northward along the Pacific Coast to see where the Spanish have left their mark; even the City of the Angels was once more of a seaport than a sprawl. One witnesses the tussle of white versus native in the place names of the Northwest coast, where a few names with unlikely consonant sequences—Kwakiutl—have held on against the ravages of Vancouver, Fraser, and Astor. The Europeans claimed the larger features for themselves, but the Indian names survive in places of beauty, mystery, and danger; more northerly still, the Russians who nearly extirpated the Aleuts have largely lost their place on the map, onomastic justice if not a judgment at Nuremberg. Hawaii, where the depredations of white missionaries and traders came late enough and where indigenous rule remained viable almost into the twentieth century, for the most part retains its traditional and euphonious place names—except for Pearl Harbor, the unfortunate epicenter of post-conquest Island history.

The seaborne environment is also shaped by language. Along with the magic that turns left to port and right to starboard once one is no longer on land, relative direction changes as well, to abaft, forward, athwart, amidships, aloft. This is compounded by the relative direction of the wind, windward and leeward, pointing (or heading) up and bearing off—unless one is in irons, trapped with the wind coming directly over the bow, making leeway perhaps, but not headway. Whether one is in a clipper ship on the high seas or a sailing dinghy on a small pond, these terms are utterly descriptive and universally understood.

The waves and wind, as well, have their own lexicons. Sailors since Homer's day have struggled to tell the color of the sea, whether wine-dark or Mediterranean blue, and waves form themselves into in rollers, combers, horse's heads, whitecaps, ripples, chop, and even rogues. Polynesian navigators found their way across the Pacific by observing the relative shape and direction of waves, and surely their vocabulary included as many words for waves as the Inuit are reputed to have for different sorts of snow. When I was a child my grandmother spoke of the "one o'clock breeze," the summer southwesterly that stirred the waters of the Peconic Bays, but in other parts of the world the wind blows in as The Doctor, as williwaws, as no'theasters, mistrals, white squalls, black squalls, and The Hawk. (The many names of the wind are often captured and bestowed upon sailing vessels themselves by their owners, either out of a desire to propitiate or else simple hubris; sailors ignore the fate of Odysseus, who belittled the power of Poseidon, at their peril.)

For sheer descriptive power few convergences of linguistic and meteorological precision have the grace of the system for classifying wind velocity devised by Admiral Sir Francis Beaufort during the Napoleonic Wars. In its simplest form, the Beaufort Scale simply describes wind speed by Force, from 1 to 12, each higher number denoting higher velocity. But the numbers fade into insignificance against the haiku-like efficiency of the names and descriptors Sir Francis bestowed upon each Force: Force 1 is a "Light Air," in which "Ripples with the appearance of scales are formed." As the wind strengthens to Force 5, a "Fresh Breeze," we observe "Moderate waves, taking a more pronounced long form; many white horses are formed." By Force 9 ("Severe Gale"), all hell is breaking loose: "High waves. Dense streaks of foam along the direction of the wind. Crests of waves begin to topple, tumble, and roll over. Spray may affect visibility." At Force 12 ("Hurricane"), hell has come: "The air is filled with foam and spray. Sea completely white with driving spray; visibility may be seriously affected." One might wish to commit the Beaufort Scale to memory, if only as a reminder that things can always be worse. Of course, use of the scale is fading out, as modern anemometers producing windspeed numbers with linear precision drive out the painterly descriptiveness of the admiral's words.

The mariner experiencing the higher end of the scale might understandably be testing the power of language in the invocation of higher powers, and religious traditions have yielded their own texts for specific maritime situations. The "Navy Hymn" beseeches the full Christian trinity to "hear us when we cry to Thee for those in peril on the sea," the pleadings of the imperiled and the anxious landsman commingled in the moment, while prayer books offer their own particular supplications on behalf of seafarers. Beneficiaries of efficacious prayers and hymns may find themselves, after long careers, retired and safe at last in places with names like Sailors' Snug Harbor, Our Island Home, or the Sailor's Rest—institutional appellations reflecting a praiseworthy eagerness to guarantee homey warmth and security to those who have been cold, homeless, and in peril. Even death has a particular argot at sea, with Davy Jones' locker awaiting the fatalistic and Fiddler's Green the fanciful. The ceremony of burial at sea provides stark images and solemn language, verbal and symbolic, whether one is committing a body wrapped in a tarpaulin or a hammock to the deep or engaging in the Viking practice of casting the body adrift on a flaming longship.

For less solemn or extreme situations, those who follow the sea are stereotypically endowed with another linguistic faculty, namely the ability to "swear like a sailor." The literature of the sea is filled with descriptions of old salts capable of uttering strings of insults and obscenities that go on for minutes at a time, although we note that virtually nowhere are these "blue streaks" transcribed. One suspects that in the high-stress environment of a ship, where the crew's survival may be very much in question, emitting a lungful of oaths is better than shiatsu massage for relieving fear and anxiety. In the autobiographical *Cradle of the Deep* by Joan Lowell, the author tells of herself as a young girl defying her captain father to listen in fascination to the swearing of sailors. However "unladylike" it might have been for the young Joan even to hear such talk, listening to the honest, authentic speech of sailors enriched the experience for her in ways that a bowdlerized, sanitized voyage would have stifled. Indeed, the sailors themselves must have appreciated the courage of the skipper's daughter and been relieved not to have had to mind their p's and q's in her presence.

The exuberance of maritime language manifests itself powerfully in the songs of seamen and the sea. The rhythmic intensity of the work chanteys to which anchors were raised, sails set, and other hard, cooperative tasks accomplished is complemented by the stories the songs tell—of love and longing for the shore, of the cruelty of captains and mates—impertinence tolerated in song—of historical moments, great ships, and great deeds. One is reminded that Homer's *Odyssey* is a song of adventure on the high seas, a tale perhaps more compelling than the boisterous "What Shall We Do with the Drunken Sailor?" but scarcely, as it was originally sung amid the wine-soaked revelry of freebooting Greeks prowling the Mediterranean for goods and reputation, more fit for drawing room society. What summer camper shouting and stamping to "Weigh! Hey! And up she rises!" around a campfire has not felt intoxicated simply by this celebration of the inebriated mariner's affront to respectability?

The music of the sea also includes works of great complexity and depth, and hardly is there a poet or composer who has not taken on an oceanic topic—descriptive, narrative, meditative, spiritual. From Handel's *Water Music* and Debussy's *La Mer* to the gripping plaint of John Masefield's "I must go down to the sea again," the attempt to capture and communicate the experience of being near or on the water in image, tone, or lyric has forever been a fundamental aspect of the human creative impulse.

The play of light on water and the stripped-to-the-bone nature of the struggle of men against the sea has inspired a visual language of water as meaningful as the poetry of words. The seascapes of Turner, the American Luminists, and Winslow Homer have taught us as much about how to look at the sea as they have drawn us into their own images, and modernists from Renoir to Marin have reduced what we see when we view moored boats or Maine islands to their extraordinarily beautiful essence, revealing the design of the world.

Whether an artist, a poet, or simply a psychic captive of some maritime narrative or picture-book of ships or whales, the child cannot but be drawn by the infinite lexicon of word and image of the sea. The richness of the ways in which our species refers to and represents the sea is perhaps an echo of the fact that our bodies, our very brains, are quite literally built of water.

V. SHORE

Atrip to the beach, the lake, or the swimming hole brightens a child's summer day. Not only is the water cooling, but in the shedding of clothes one undergoes a liberation that harks back to the most primeval human experience. Something about the water wants us to become simple animals, to become fish, once again: naked, careless, responding to the breath and tug of wind and current. Beachgoers array themselves primitively, moving their bodies to follow the sun like a field of plants heliotroping through the cycle of the day. The beach is a living diorama of phylogeny.

At the water's edge social conventions are ignored or abrogated. Along with throwing off layers of clothing, bathers (or sunbathers) reject even urban notions of social space, packing their exposed bodies onto the sand or the picnic area in densities that would be wholly unacceptable in any other kind of private recreation. Marking off personal territory with blankets, towels, and the ubiquitous folding chair, people at waterside are content to share in ways that might make behavioral psychologists scratch their heads. The relative vastness of the water, its relative coolness, absorbs excess human energy and heat, psychically extending each individual's social space into its tranquil

40

depths. Even a crowded public swimming pool can miraculously dissipate the grumpy potential energy of its users on a hot day.

Those interested in the purity and authenticity of children's exposure to the natural world might scoff at the typical experience of the American beachgoing child, where the destination is a crowded shore with a "safe" area marked by floats and guarded by red bathingsuit-clad avatars (on raised thrones), each aspiring to perfect human form like so many models awaiting a call from Michelangelo or Rodin. Perhaps littered with bottle tops and cigarettebutts—occasionallby medical waste cast up by the waves—this bit of nature might have little to recommend it other than the presence of water.

But children can find, even in the most aesthetically challenged setting, things to amuse and enlighten. With feeble plastic shovels and tiny buckets, they indulge the human instinct for digging and building, discovering the water table as well as differences in the types of sand, stones, and shells that make up the beach. The most jaded of children will still have a small collection of interesting or pretty shells and stones to remove from bathing suit pockets at bedtime, proof of the human proclivity to touch, to feel what is strange and to somehow make it a part of ourselves; I had almost written "possess," but that is too conscious and too crude. The child who picks up a scallop shell does not want so much to possess it as to incorporate its strange, symmetrical beauty into his or her own being.

At the very point where water meets land, the child (and the adult) finds much to see. Small fish dart with electronic speed through the shallows, appearing and disappearing in their swarms as if controlled by an invisible switch. Perhaps frogs conceal themselves in the grasses of a still corner of a cove, or turtles take the sun on a rock—

all creatures to be observed, carefully held by the quick and the brave, and returned to their habitat. Shells in their multitudes attract the eye, and gathering a variety can activate the sorting and classifying mind of the young naturalist. Even the plants have things to teach: poison ivy's hard lesson is one, but so is the surprising sharpness of many kinds of beach grass and the briny succulence of saltwater pickle. While plants at the water's edge are best not picked—their niche is precarious enough as it is—they can be felt and looked at and smelled, their leaves counted, the insects upon them observed at close hand. There is a rich harvest for the mind, at least.

The shore offers a feast for all the senses. The smell of fish, of vegetation moldering in a marsh, of salt in the air, even of the exhaust fumes of passing vessels—these are rich scents to be sorted and savored in present experience and in memory, ready in the future to trigger pleasant associations. The natural hygroscopy of skin measures for us the ambient humidity: dry days by the waterside are a sun-dried gift, while hazy, hot, and humid periods pass with miasmic slowness. The sounds of wave, wind, boat, and bird give fullness to our time, completing our envelopment.

The same opportunities abound for the close observation of nature and nature's patterns along a rocky or wooded shore. Hours may be spent exploring the tidal pools that form among the rocks, working carefully along ledges slippery with algae and wrack, or simply watching the sublime minuet of the irresistible force of great waves encountering the immovability of a rockbound coast.

In much of inland North America certain trees, comforting and welcoming as old friends to those who know them, announce the presence of water, their lushness marking the course of creeks and rivers. In pre-Columbian and pioneer times, stands of willow, mesquite, and alder stood as beacons inviting humans to fertile floodplains and bottom lands, and they still bespeak vitality.

We may be hard-wired to spot water, but as a species we seem equally determined to make our mark upon each and every watercourse. Whenever man has stopped to eat, drink, or procreate, there the careful—and open-minded—observer can find illustrative remnants of man's relationship with this environment, from Indian shell mounds and arrowheads to the contemporary effluvia of illicit beer-drinking or love-making. Other, perhaps more significant artifacts appear in the most surprising places—here the wreckage of a dam, its concrete bound with old automobile frames; there a fence running into the water and indicating a change in course, perhaps within living memory.

The work of animals is another thing: beaver dams and lodges, the footprints of wading birds in shallow reaches, the shining vee of the wake of a mink or weasel swimming in haste away from the human intruder, nests and burrows along the banks from which birds, or snakes, or small rodents may (or may not) appear.

All this is available, too, to the observer on the edge of much larger bodies of water, on a proportionate scale. The natural and unnatural detritus along a beach or shoreline can teach much about animal, vegetable, and human processes. The plastic juice bottle with the label in Spanish washed up on a Long Island beach, the strange shell suspended from the seaweed balloon that has carried it to shore, the strange bird, so different from all the others racing back and forth across the beach—all excite curiosity and wonder, the same wonder with which the child searches the wrack and her imagination for a message in a bottle, or longs to send her own.

The littered shoreline offers great possibilities for stewardship. The child given a bag and a stretch of beach to clear of human-created waste will begin to understand some of the darker lessons of human behavior as well as to see immediately the positive results of even a little action; perhaps that child will develop an aversion to plastic packaging that will one day grow into a commitment to change the world. On some rivers environmentalists have created the job of "riverkeeper." Self-designated caretakers may be one of our last hopes for undoing the human depredations of our waterways, and each beach, pond, or stream to which we can give the gift of "keeping" is one potential bastion against catastrophe.

I have above made several references to shorebirds, which comprise one of the attractions that bring our attention to the sea. Whether we are looking at the majesty of a great pelagic bird like an albatross or the swarming of gulls around a fishing boat or even the comical rushing of "LGBs"—little gray birds such as sand pipers, turnstones, and the like—back and forth across a beach, there is something about the appearance and behavior of water birds that compels the eye and lifts the spirit in ways that only a few totemic "land birds"—bluebirds, robins, or hawks—can match. Perhaps it is because birds on or over water are easier to spot against the relatively monochromatic ground of the sea, lake, or river. Or perhaps there is something more elemental about shorebirds, whose bodies and eggs have been hunted for human sustenance and decoration since time immemorial and whose very presence is a harbinger, to the soul long at sea, of land, and safety. The soul, too, can be transported by the cries of those birds most especially associated with the waters of the world—the loon, the kingfisher, the tern, among others.

Three vantage points are available to one who would look upon seashore: from the land, upon the water, or in it. As a species our vision is drawn toward water from land, and we cannot refrain from making a watercourse of any size the center of our idea of the picturesque. But to look from the water to the shore reverses things. On a pleasant, calm day—of Beaufort Force perhaps below 3 or 4—we can enjoy the view of the edge of the lake or harbor from the seat of a canoe, kayak, or small motorboat. Plodding along at walking speed, we can look at length upon the nature of the shoreline and of the dwellings and other signs of human habitation. Some observers wrap (or warp) themselves obsessively in the business of closely examining the homes of others, comparing window placement, building materials, landscaping, paint jobs, and even the numbers of bathrooms (as evidenced by the number of vent-stacks in the roof)—the art of people-watching by observation of their nests.

Other shorewatchers take pleasure in the sudden or even familiar thrill of coming upon the beauty of a natural spot, or an arrangement of the human (a moored boat, perhaps) against a natural backdrop. A ferry ride to a cherished destination is among the most exhilarating kinds of shore watching: gazing from the deck as familiar places and objects grow distinct and then larger, more real; joyous associations suffusing the spirit until, with the gentle bump of the ship entering its slip, one experiences physical union with the beloved. Artists in such locales find a steady market for paintings and sketches that attempt to capture these images, to distill the embodiment and archetype of places in the heart.

In the sea itself is yet another matter. The swimmer sees the land and sea together, whether in the swirling chaos of surf or the placidity of flatwater. Even those who only wade in the shallows, like great pink and brown shorebirds, experience the sea in a way fundamentally distinct from their own experience standing on the shore a few yards off. When one is wet, the circuit between body and environment is made more efficient, sensation conducted more directly. Afloat, gravity is for once held in abeyance, the body governed by new laws whose study becomes natural only when one can relax and feel their subtle power. Freud spoke of the "oceanic feeling," of an empowering connectedness like floating amid the potential goodwill of humanity. The contented swimmer floating on his or her back in a calm sea, eyes shut against the dazzling sun, knows this feeling literally; for some, even a bathtub can provide it.

The art of moving in water, whether with a graceful, schooled stroke, a childish paddle, or the cork-like bobbing of those who enjoy being lifted and set down by the passing waves, is probably more ancient than we believe; the "ocean bathing" craze of the nineteenth century that has come down to our own day merely institutionalized the individual practice of the ages. We envy the sponge and pearl divers of Greece and Japan who, without equipment, effortlessly inhabit the medium of the creatures they hunt, and it is almost impossible not to watch the natural swimming of children at home in the water, whose grace we would want to capture—perhaps just once more—in our own movements. At the same time we are told that fishermen and mariners the world over choose not to learn the art of swimming so as to abbreviate futile struggles in the aftermath of misadventure far from shore; one admires the sentiment, perhaps, but at the same time one ponders how they can so preemptively abandon hope.

Perhaps these same fishermen and mariners behold the shore with a more profound joy than the casual swimmer or boater can ever muster; when the outline of home port begins to resolve itself into familiar features and houses, what relief! Perhaps this relief is what invigorates our sense of those seaside communities most notable not only for their rich smell of water and fish, but also for the picturesque vessels tied to their piers and anchored in their harbors. For many humans, looking at boats, as much as messing about in them, is the essence of the sea.

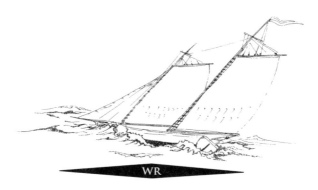

WR

VI. Tall Ships

The flack who "re-purposed" John Masefield's descriptive phrase to characterize and publicize the first grand commemorative movable feast of sailing ships in 1976 managed to create the perfect landlubber's image of "the tall ship and a star to steer her by" for which the poet pined. The worldwide gathering of "Tall Ships" that made its stately procession along the seaports of America's East Coast coincident with the national bicentennial was indeed notable not only for the sheer number but for the vertical majesty of the vessels involved.

As a child in the fifties and sixties, I, too, had pined for a tall ship and a star, a craving that was at that time almost impossible to gratify. Fortunately, I was able to glimpse the Coast Guard Academy training vessel *Eagle* a couple of times, and my mother took me to Mystic Seaport to walk upon the (then) firmly grounded deck of the whaler *Charles W. Morgan*. I knew that in England *Cutty Sark* and HMS *Victory* were on display, but I sorrowed over the otherwise complete, or so I thought, demise of the Age of Sail. My heart yearned to refloat the two abandoned schooners that once marked the tourist's arrival in Wiscasset, Maine, and the thought of taking one of the windjammer cruises I saw advertised in magazines

48

filled me with awe and longing. To have joined the crew of Irving and Exy Johnson's *Yankee* for the adventures chronicled in old *National Geographic* magazines was my highest aspiration.

But fifty years ago, the Age of Sail was over, at least in the material sense. It might have been possible to restore the old schooners of Wiscasset, but finding skilled laborers willing or even able to do the work would have been nearly impossible. Elsewhere on Earth, new materials and increasingly efficient internal-combustion engines had put paid to any notion of making money by building or operating large sailing vessels.

But the Age of Sail was immanent in the souls and minds of many. The market for nautical fiction and maritime history remained steady and even began to grow in some categories, and the sheer romance of the sailing ship era continued to play on the hearts of those who still thrilled at Melville's writing about sailing (even more than in contemplation of Ahab's psyche or Queequeg's tattoos) or who were read to from dog-eared copies of Arthur Ransome's *Swallows and Amazons* books. The high seas, the sounds and sights and smells of canvas sails and wooden ships (and iron men, as they had it) had made an indelible impression upon the culture, and the culture was not about to give it up. They were legion who longed to look upon such vessels.

By the end of the 1980s, the Age of Sail, and the age of wooden boats, had come again. Derelict sailing ships from around the globe were under restoration by a new cadre of craftspersons; the art of wooden boat design, building, and repair was being taught in specialized courses across the maritime world; and sail training programs provided cadets and paying customers with learning experiences that once again included windlasses, ratlines, footropes, and the smell of Stockholm tar.

A few devotees of this resurgent fleet, assembled for reasons not quite commercial nor quite for pleasure alone, came to their interest from successful but unsatisfying work in other areas. As they raised their own level of seamanship to new standards and learned the skills required to construct a large vessel from living wood, they brought with them the precision and work ethic that had driven them in careers in business and finance, and they brought with them also their own capital and a fierce enthusiasm that attracted still more of it. The new Age of Sail might not be about making money, but it would not be about losing it, either. Better still, career-changing shipbuilders and mariner wannabes were persuasive not only in garnering the funds to finance their new passion but also in finding and enlisting the support of the lost generation of master mariners and master shipwrights who could teach them what they would need to know.

For some of the neophytes discovering the Tall Ships, as practically any vessel powered by sail and larger than a medium-sized yacht came to be called, the lure was in the adventure, the risk, and the shipboard camaraderie. Others possessed a sensibility that had always gravitated toward boats and the sea, the kind of teenagers who could identify several dozen kinds of small sailboat classes by a glance at their hulls alone or who could knowingly differentiate the designs of one Herreshoff (members of the famous yacht-designing clan from Rhode Island) from another.

These are the young people for whom the romance and majesty and mystery of the sea are made concrete in the curves of a beautiful hull, a well-set sail, or a motorboat with classic lines crashing through waves with confidence and power. For them, the boating magazines at the newsstand have the allure of sex: catalogs of possibility and fuel for endless fantasy and speculation. They fill their school notebooks with drawings of boats, some rendered with architectural precision and others sketched with lines of furious action. In one another's company, a rare enough circumstance through childhood, they share obscure fantasies of performance and aesthetics.

Perhaps these youngsters are fortunate enough to be able to enact their dreams, to sail or row or motor, and to hone their skills in their preferred medium under the tutelage of some elder. Their love of the sea (even if their sea is only a pond) will be consummated by their actions, but at sea their greatest joy is in looking upon the multitude of other vessels, large and small, and cultivating their appreciation—perhaps more than a bit promiscuous—of all the ships and boats. Whether covetous or generous, their love will at some point fall on, perhaps permanently, the large vessels of the Age of Sail.

The love of these boats and ships for their own sake is a powerful liquor that works deep magic. Some may be enamored of the schooners, whether the great Grand Bankers like *Bluenose* or the smaller, tidier designs of an Atkin or an Alden. Others will fall in love with the almost unbelievable complexity and beauty of clipper ships, the pinnacle of the sailing shipbuilder's art, capable of enormous speed and carrying so many sails, controlled by so many lines, that to know their workings in detail is a life's task. For others, perhaps in the grip of the many authors who churn out high-quality fiction of the days of sailing navies, the fast frigates or the multi-decked ships of the line of the Napoleonic era are the love interest; for them, the USS *Constitution* ("Old Ironsides") or HMS *Victory* are Holy Grails, objects of a desirability that passeth understanding.

Opportunities abound for those who would set their hands to the building or renovation of such vessels. Special schools in scenic coastal communities and community colleges in maritime states offer instruction in the art of building wooden boats and in the sometimes more challenging arts of making them new. A whole vocabulary of tools and rarefied skills attends these tasks, from spuds to spiling, and the workplace itself is a kind of sensory paradise: the smell of woodchips and turpentine and glue, the luster of golden timbers fresh-sawn or -planed, the whine of saws biting into baulks of exotic woods, and the muffled thud of mallets persuading hand-shaped planks into their proper places.

If building is not enough, then the places where young people can learn the skills and teamwork involved in managing a large sailing vessel are many. Some such programs focus on the character-building aspects of shiphandling: managing fear, working with others, living in confined spaces, following orders. Other programs are built around the development of skills—seamanship, pure and simple. A few institutions use sailing vessels as a site for educational programs, primarily in the marine sciences or as part of a larger effort to expand environmental awareness and expertise. Exotic ports of call and destinations are de rigueur, in no small measure because tropical theaters of operation offer longer cruising seasons; yet no photogenic seaport town or stunning maritime vista, north or south, goes unvisited for long. Arguably the legacy of Irving Johnson and the *Yankee* tradition, the Tall Ships of the burgeoning sail-training fleet provide precisely the fix that my younger self and so many other boat-obsessed children were craving.

This is not to say that the young can only set sail in Tall Ships. The parallel development of "small ships" in the last few decades has created an extraordinary number of boaters. The number of community and club instructional sailing programs has increased, some devoted to developing racing expertise but others focused on giving students the competence to derive pleasure from recreational sailing. On places like Nantucket Island, for example, where by the 1950s a three-century tradition of working under canvas had been supplanted by an ethos in which only wealthy summer residents sailed, the community sailing program has had a democratizing effect, putting year-round islanders and their children back at the tiller.

Lately oar- and paddle-powered vessels appear even more frequently than canoes on the roof-racks of family vans and sedans headed for a waterside vacation. Inexpensive molded kayaks built to accommodate varying degrees of paddling expertise are everywhere, used as fishing platforms, for providing on-the-water workouts, and as tools of exploration on rivers, lakes, and coastal waterways. Rowing boats built for open water provide serious exercise as well as a way to poke around into enticing pieces of coastline, and ambitious paddlers and oarsmen can compete in a growing number of distance races, like the annual Blackburn Challenge in Massachusetts, in which boaters commemorate a harrowing survival tale by rowing or paddling more than twenty miles; unlike Thomas Blackburn's 1883 ordeal, the race occurs in summer. Where its namesake lost most of his fingers to frostbite, participants in the race are rewarded with a clambake.

The shelves of any large bookstore will yield any number of books on do-it-yourself small-boat building, offering the would-be shipwright the instruction necessary to create anything from a simple plywood rowboat to an Aleut-style kayak with its wooden frame lashed together with, in place of sinew, polyester cord. Ambitious home boatbuilders have created beautiful renditions of classic designs in their backyards, and there has even been a brief craze for hulls of ferrocement among amateur builders. Many of these projects eventually involve whole families, giving children the opportunity to develop a sense of craftsmanship in a context that demands full attention and responsibility: The birdhouse project in shop class can tolerate improper measurement and sloppy joinery that the hull and rigging of a boat in which the builder will go to sea cannot.

In a previous chapter I wrote of the visual language that artists have developed to represent the sea, and there is no less poetic a visual language understood by those who love to look at boats and spoken by those who design them. From the linear dignity of Great Lakes ore boats to eel-like submarines and bulbous ice-breakers to the drop-dead-gorgeous shapes of iconic yacht designs—the work of Nathanael and L. Francis Herreshoff, the Concordia yawl, the motorsailers of William Hand, the powerboats of Chris-Craft and Lyman, the canoes of William Rushton, and even the Laser sailboat—there is a sweetness of line and a balance of form that boat-watchers understand and even need. No girl from Ipanema has evoked as many "aaahs" in her lifetime as any incarnation of L. Francis Herreshoff's Rozinante yawl design or a well-maintained triple-cockpit Chris-Craft runabout from 1931. Even the most obtuse landsman sees the beauty of these designs, in which form flows smoothly from function even if the latter is only vaguely understood.

Which brings us full circle back to the Tall Ships themselves. On parade, entering a cheering, hooting harbor as part of a cultural or historical celebration, the Tall Ships under full sail are works of art, and their crews on deck or arrayed in the rigging have worked overtime applying complex skills to make them look their best. Sailing under many flags from around the world, these ships are widely touted as ambassadors of goodwill, and, when they are tied to the wharves of a public space amid great festivities, they invoke the possibility of a better, more peaceful, and more understanding world.

But above all the Tall Ships are ambassadors from another time and indeed from another aesthetic. The young men and women who crew them, and the older seamen who command them and who have devoted their lives to maintaining and passing down traditions of seamanship, are sharing a world in which the timeless discipline and the glory of the sea are made manifest, a world in which "doing it right" is the only way. When things are done right, as we learn from navigating tall ships and small ships alike, we connect with a world that in its breadth and spectacle allows us to see a bit more of our own potential.

VII. Captain

Let us return to the image, from Chapter II, of the child making a first solo voyage around the harbor in a small sailboat. We behold a couple of anxious adults, perhaps an instructor and a parent, watching closely as the tiny boat zigs and zags, outward bound from the pier. The set of the sail, the position of the rudder, are keenly noted. The small helmsperson, outsize in a yellow personal flotation device (the children are taught never to refer to them as "life jackets"; they guarantee only that the wearer floats, not lives), wiggles the tiller, a bit too ardently, but the boat continues on its course. A couple of maneuvers, a messy landing fended off without comment by the proud adults, and the boat is made fast. With a poker face, the young captain furls the sail and steps on shore, the sailor home from the sea. Someone says, "Well done, skipper!"

Skipper! Captain. Master and commander. Boss. What child does not long for some acknowledgment of readiness to take control of his or her own life, even in the smallest degree? When the instructional boating program bestows this rating on the child, perhaps years before the child would be eligible for a driver's license or even be permitted by parents to take public transportation alone, the message is clear: this child has achieved a degree of competence that, in the considered opinion of others experienced in the same arts, will ensure his or her safety in managing a small boat in certain, narrowly described circumstances. The transatlantic voyage is yet a ways off, but this Saturday's junior race? Absolutely.

It may not be a sailboat, and the situation may not be quite so formal, but at some point all children growing up around the water and small boats achieve their first voyage alone. Perhaps the oars or paddle are still clumsily handled, but the child learns to make the passage from Point A to Point B with increasing efficiency and grace, learning with each journey more about how to manage wind, waves, traffic, and perhaps a changing tide. (As of this writing, the younger child learning to operate a motorboat may need adult supervision until a certain age or until the child has actually passed a written test to earn licensure; in some states, underage children may not operate a motorboat under any circumstances, not even with a parent's hand upon the child's shoulder. This emphasis on safety is laudable, especially as jet-skis and other small boats become faster and more lethal with technical development; the dinghy with a three-horsepower outboard is no longer the norm. One laments the loss, not so much of the opportunity for children to learn to operate motorboats safely at an early age, but rather of the world in which such vessels were fewer, slower, and arguably safer.)

It is not entirely coincidental that the symbol of Rhode Island, the Ocean State, is the "Independent Man." The political contrariety of citizens of the last of the original thirteen states to ratify the Constitution (with a few quibbles, no less) aside, the idea that people whose lives are spent in close proximity to the sea might develop their personal takes on matters of all kinds is not far-fetched.

No two trips upon the water, no matter what the body of water might be, are exactly alike. Minute variations in conditions require minor adjustments to speed and course, always based on the judgment of the sailor (or paddler or oarsman or driver) in charge—and someone must be in charge. Patterns may emerge, as similar conditions call for similar behaviors from trip to trip, but there are simply no two absolutely identical trips. (Regular ferry riders will observe this phenomenon, perhaps to their surprise.) The sea—or the river, or the pond—is an ever-changing problem, and it is up to the commander, the skipper, the captain, to apply experience and wisdom to this problem and create a solution: a course, at a given rate of speed.

As I write this chapter, a fierce line squall—if I read my Beaufort Scale properly, a Severe Gale—has been making its way down the large lake our rented cottage overlooks. As the storm reached its peak, with windows crashing, doors slamming, and papers flying off tables, a small cabin cruiser, perhaps a bit over thirty feet in length, set out from the bay where its owner had probably stopped for lunch. Almost instantly exposed to the full fury of the rising wind, the little vessel ceased to be a pleasant, reliable portable habitat and became a ship in a storm. The owner, for we tend to impute proprietorship to the operators of such boats, had suddenly the need to become its captain. On his or her judgment alone rested, quite literally, the safety of those aboard. Perhaps they did not appreciate the skill required, but as I watched the boat laboring upwind, away from the granite cliffs against which it otherwise must surely have been dashed, I found myself admiring, and rooting for, the captain. Whoever it was had had sense enough to see the storm approaching, raise the anchor, and get under way before the squall arrived, and they seemed aware, perhaps instinctively or perhaps by training, of the need to keep the bow pointed into the wicked wind and to apply enough power to make headway but not to lose control. By the time the boat had moved out of sight, I was confident that those aboard would make it safely to the nearby harbor. Aboard the vessel, the captain was climbing perhaps the steepest learning curve of his or her life, and the presence of family or friends aboard must only have sharpened the senses and inspired an even greater sense of the requirement to apply every bit of knowledge and wisdom available. If the owner had not been exactly a captain before—a real landlubber on such a vessel might have self-identified as the "driver"—by the time the boat was making fast to the wharf at the marina up the way, the dockhand's likely greeting, "You must have had a time of it, eh, skipper?" would have affirmed for the shaken operator that he or she has earned a captain's stripes—in a half-hour or less.

Had it been a child in a rowboat (or myself in my kayak, even), the learning curve would have been steeper, and the outcome perhaps less positive. We do not expect to find ourselves in challenging situations (and we will hold off from faulting the cruiser's skipper for failing to have heeded the weather forecasts), but when as it happens we do, when we go to sea, the learning is immediate and intense, the lesson often impossible to ignore or avoid. As captains of our vessels, large and small, we all earn our stripes.

In the previous chapter we referred to sail-training programs, especially those focused on character and leadership development. Even in the waning days of the true Age of Sail, mariners aboard steamships were aware of the skill and "command sense" deficits among sailors who had never served under sail. Because the only way to make a sailing vessel move is through a purposeful manipulation of the rig, and because in the merchant fleet and the military alike trial-and-error had long since given way to a known set of best practices, sail training became part of some national seamanship courses—the United States Coast Guard Academy, for example—early on. The United States Naval Academy at Annapolis (the yachting center of the Chesapeake Bay, aside from the presence of the Academy) and the U.S. Merchant Marine Academy at Kings Point, New York, encourage cadets to master small-boat sailing and racing in the belief that the sea-sense and judgment required to handle small sailing vessels have concomitant utility in commanding larger vessels, or even entire fleets.

Above all what is required for command is confidence, and in many cases experience alone can bring this. The Outward Bound program, offering courses around the world focused in building confidence and good values through outdoor experiences, began during World War II as a training program for merchant sailors in the period when German U-boats were having spectacular success in sinking Allied shipping and when the mortality rate of merchant seamen was disturbingly and unexpectedly high. Sailors who were taught a few proven survival skills, it turned out, were more likely to survive sinkings than their totally untrained counterparts, and the program's founders knew that the true value of the training was in giving participants the confidence that calamity was survivable. A number of the Outward Bound program's current courses involve lengthy journeys under sail and oar in large open boats, where students learn a great deal about seamanship and themselves, and from which many emerge with a newfound belief in their own capacity to succeed in arenas far from the sea—even if their lives have heretofore been less than stellar or happy.

A stock element of the literature of the sea,

fact and fiction, is the question of fitness for command. Captain Bligh of the HMS *Bounty* has become a byword for cruelty, a nautical Simon Legree, although the actual record shows that Bligh was a successful commander (at least at sea; his term as a governor in the penal colonies of Australia was also marked by mutiny) who managed what may have been the greatest open-boat voyage ever, over 2,600 miles, with his fellow *Bounty* exiles after the mutiny. Captain Queeg of the Herman Wouk's fictional destroyer USS *Caine* is the very model of the paranoid boss, an inwardly focused madman whose delusions may yet have been necessary to his effectiveness. Captain Smith of the *Titanic*, who went down with his ship, has taken his place under the umbrella of hubris we associate with the "unsinkable" vessel, while Melville's Ahab, as we have already seen, is a handy all-purpose symbol of the self-absorbed lunatic who controls the destiny of his crew. It is virtually a rule of maritime service that a captain whose vessel is lost or damaged is held guilty until proven innocent, a situation that has eternally damned Joseph Hazelwood of the *Exxon Valdez*, which ran aground and dumped its own ocean of crude oil into the sensitive waters of the Gulf of Alaska, in public memory. A few years ago the author of a book on a whaling disaster that proceeded to cannibalism and murder before its few survivors were rescued was surprised to find himself recruited to present his thoughts on the effective command of nineteenth-century whaling vessels to top executives of an investment banking firm; the story, the CEO believed, had relevance for today's captains of finance, too. (Whether the CEO was for or against cannibalism has not been resolved.)

Notable in this context is the modest but persistent popularity of series fiction focusing on the exploits of naval officers from the Age of Sail. Patrick O'Brian's Jack Aubrey is catapulted to command in the first of the highly literate cascade of adventures that feature Aubrey and his physician-spy "particular friend," Stephen Maturin; and C. S. Forester's Horatio Hornblower, Alexander Kent's Richard Bolitho, Richard Woodman's Nathaniel Drinkwater, and Dudley Pope's Lord Nicholas Ramage all work their way swiftly up the ranks of the Royal Navy during the Napoleonic Wars to achieve command. A theme in all these stories is the isolation that comes with ultimate authority; Aubrey must withhold his concerns even from Maturin at various points. A second theme is the consequence of failure; each protagonist has at least one sobering brush with court-martial as well as many with death.

If we return to our young sailor taking that first sail alone, we know that he or she is indeed experiencing independence and self-reliance in a life-changing way. But we (and the tyro skipper) also know that a still greater challenge of command awaits: the first time in charge of a boat with a crew. With others at his or her command, the newly fledged captain must be responsible not only for the sum total of all judgment regarding the operation of the vessel, but also for issuing orders—a sobering word in itself—that will, in naval parlance, "make it so." The captain needs the knowledge and the conviction to transform his or her ideas into effective words that will persuade others unquestioningly to swift and proper action.

Instructional boating programs in camps and at community organizations and yacht clubs know the power of the dilemma (as opposed to the true crisis) as a teaching tool. The consequences belong to the captain; whether becalmed or stalled in the middle of the harbor or lake, a paddle lost or a rudder malfunctioning, only the commander's words and deeds (including the perfectly acceptable option of soliciting ideas from the crew, knowing that the skipper must make the final decision as to what must be done) will bring the boat back to shore. Rescue must be made only as a last resort, or else the chance for real learning is lost. The resolution may take time, and the youngsters may return cold, wet, hungry, and out of sorts—but they have done it themselves, and the captain has met the first obligation of command by bringing vessel and crew home safe and sound. A hot meal and a round of restorative beverages will soon set all to rights, as such have ever soothed the souls of sailors home from the sea. Whether on pizza or roast pig, root beer or rum, the nautical appetite can be well satisfied—and wise indeed is the captain who knows just when and how to issue the order for the extra round (or the extra slice) by way of rewarding good service in hard circumstances.

Young or old, while at sea the skipper is indeed the master of his fate, the captain of her soul. In few other situations can a person find himself or herself so totally in charge (and indeed, so totally alone). At some point most human beings long for such a degree of control over their lives, and more than a few are not shy about extending that control to others. The child weaving the pram among the buoys and boats in a small harbor is no less alert to the degree to which the outcome is in his or her own hands than the captain of the aircraft carrier steaming toward a war zone or the master of the supertanker working his way into a busy roadstead—or the operator of a cabin cruiser in a sudden storm. With skill, self-assurance, a modicum of luck, and enough tutelage to be able draw upon the traditions and wisdom of the sea, each will make port with vessel, crew, and cargo intact. The fearful trip will at last be done.

WR

VIII. Crew

Underrated in a society focused on each individual achieving primacy in everything from school to sports to business to volunteerism is the art of following. At sea, however, this art is every bit as crucial as the judgment of the commander, and a part of the apprenticeship of every sailor, no matter how small-scale the enterprise, is learning how and when to follow orders.

Much has been written recently of the governance of pirate ships. The old model of bad people following avaricious leaders in pursuit of booty and gratification has been refined as our understanding of the "democratic" nature of Early Modern-era Western piracy has expanded. Pirates followed a leader who could lead them to what they needed, and mechanisms for deposing an unsatisfactory leader (other than by a forced walk on the plank) often involved actual voting, of which we see a remnant in the "Black Spot" levied against Billy Bones in *Treasure Island*; clubs use essentially the same system for excluding unwanted members. Anyone who wanted to go on the pirate account on the Spanish Main was making a conscious decision to engage in an enterprise in which the quality of leadership was guaranteed, at least theoretically, to be relatively high. The stakes, of course, were life and death, but the prudent member of a pirate crew made sure to have more than a little say in the decision-making hierarchy of his (or her, it must be remembered) ship.

Mutiny and piracy lie at the outer fringes of an exploration of the qualities of "crewship" or "followership," a role for which our me-first society does not even have a felicitous word. The stakes and requirements for those acting in support roles at sea tend to be reduced to several areas, each of which has an important relationship to the broadest definition of being effectively human. These include teamwork, learning to follow orders, and the ability to engage with the common purpose and common values.

Few activities put a greater premium on teamwork, cooperation, and collaboration than being in a boat. Even a two-person vessel requires both leading and following: someone sets the stroke in a double-shell or a double canoe or kayak, and the second person must follow in precise unison. One person must determine direction, and the other must adjust his or her actions to make the direction-change smoothly. Even when the paddlers or rowers are periodically switching positions and roles, the follower must follow, exactly. (An entertaining aspect of watching young canoeists learn to paddle is to observe the process whereby close friends negotiate their way into "stroke" and "steer" roles, a process that invariably begins with the canoe describing several circles, followed by a snake-like course that gradually straightens to a line as they paddlers come to understand, then yield, then accept their several roles, "captain" and "crew.")

The teamwork aspect of being a good crew member plays out in the organizational traditions of the sea. Both the day and the crews themselves are divided into watches, "shifts" necessary to keep a vessel sailing through twenty-four hours and themselves under the orders of an "officer of the watch." Other mechanisms—chanteys and chants to maintain rhythm, for example—help to coordinate work requiring the multiplied labor of many people; the coxswain of a racing shell is merely performing a distilled version of the work of the chanteyman aboard a ship, calling the work cadence and adjusting for changing conditions.

Recently there has been considerable interest in the business community in the "crew team" as a model for effective collaboration. For some tens of thousands of dollars, an executive group can spend a few days at a rowing center learning teamwork and ultimately competing, boat for boat, against their peers. The object lessons are apparently worth the cost to the corporations that have embraced such methods, and the metaphor is perhaps sound, albeit limited.

For children, especially for those whose lives have been tainted by experiences that make it difficult for them to trust others, being part of a crew—of a shell or of a sail-training ship—can be the lesson in relying on others that begins the process of developing the deeper faith in one's own judgment and one's capacity to know when it is all right to put oneself in the care, or under the command, of others. While school and community sports are supposed to teach this balance between self-reliance and teamwork, being in a boat whose direction and motion is driven only by the brains and muscles of a group creates a deeper bond, perhaps, than all but the most humanely coached and fortuitously configured (for example) soccer teams.

The mutual dependency of crew members and their common dependence on the good judgment of the captain mirrors, simply and explicitly, many of life's situations. The figure of speech, "all in the same boat" expresses the typicality, even banality, of the human condition projected as shared circumstances. Somewhere deep in the general unconscious we envision ourselves, particularly in times of stress, as if afloat, part not of a whole but of a smaller group, bound by some unspoken tie and working, together, to reach "the other side." Like the crew team, we can do this only by pulling together. In joy we may experience an oceanic feeling of universal connectedness, but in sorrow or fear we look desperately for our fellows in a more restricted circle, and perhaps we even pray for the guidance of a divine captain.

To be effective as a crew member, one must be versed in the fundamental skills of operating the vessel and in the more general skills we call seamanship. In teaching "crewship" to children, we often begin with line-handling and gear-stowing before progressing to steering, inculcating by example and instruction the proper vocabulary and the development of the muscle memory, the understanding of cause and effect, and the sense of order required to work quickly and tidily at sea. That the consequences for failure are somewhat higher than, say, doing a poor job drying the dishes, results in the task being completed with a bit more engagement, a bit more care. Families who boat together and who pass along a love of the activity from generation to generation have managed to make learning these skills, as well as acting in the "subservient" role of a crew member, rewarding and fun; the pirate captain would be envious. As children grow older and as the scope of the boating enterprise expands, the teaching-and-learning process enlarges proportionately.

A not-insignificant aspect of being effective crew involves having internalized the core values and beliefs of the "culture," whether this is the microculture of a tiny vessel or the overarching values, beliefs, and traditions of the larger maritime world. Coleridge's "Rime of the Ancient Mariner" hinges on the heedless action of a common sailor who, in killing an albatross, violates a core taboo of sailors offshore. The suffering this action calls down not just upon the seaman but also upon his fellows demonstrates, among other things, what happens when a selfish crew member flouts the regular order of things—a result as dire as if the sailor had purposely cut a hole in the ship's hull or sliced through a crucial line. The traditions and values of the sea matter. Cruise-ship passengers still hear an echo of this in "crossing the line" festivities, featuring a mischievous King Neptune and his court, held when a vessel passes the Equator; first-timers undergo a mild, comical humiliation, which they refuse at their— and by tradition, their vessel's—peril.

Adherence to sustaining values learned and reinforced as a member of a crew can give meaning to life long after the voyage is done, and in adult life we are likely to encounter enthusiastic partisans of this or that institution whose love is based on some significant experience working with others with others on water. Prep schools and colleges find in their ex-rowers many of their most devoted and active alumnae and alumni, and in crew programs the convergence of values of school and sport inspires participants to submit to a physical discipline that non-rowers consider insane—but a regime apparently remembered in a way that generates unequaled open-heartedness toward the institution. Among the most passionate of summer campers are those whose longest-lasting and most intimate friendships were (or are being) built sailing and canoeing. Those who have not shared these experiences may feel envious; the others have indeed been to a special place that the rest of us have been denied, and our loss is palpable in their presence.

Loyalty to others, to an institution, to an idea, and above all to a commander, though it is a suspect virtue in some quarters, has ever been fundamental to the effective functioning of a crew. "The captain and the loyal crew" has become a cliché because of the power of the adjective. The captain must be able to expect not only instant and correct obedience but, more importantly, willing obedience, especially when in difficult circumstances— dire straits, perhaps—the captain's orders run counter to the intuition of crew members or when the captain's selection of a narrow and hazardous path to success might cause less committed, less loyal, crew to dither or disagree. In familiar circumstances the young person learns loyalty to a "captain," a parent or cousin or aunt, by seeing that person's judgment confirmed: the canoe makes it through the stretch of rapids, the heeling sailboat ceases the unpleasant rocking motion, turning the motorboat into the wake of the passing ship is indeed the safest course. The child becomes the passionate devotee of the capable elder, a loyal crew member on any subsequent voyage.

In the naval and merchant services, the most terrible crime, carrying the most severe penalty, is active disloyalty: mutiny. Two hundred years on, the story of the *Bounty* still grips readers and moviegoers, and in any hierarchical organization—office politics come to mind— the hint of rebellion or a failure to follow orders is designated "mutiny" only in whispered tones and in the most extreme circumstances. It is the first and foremost duty of the crew of any vessel to obey the lawful orders of the commander. The interpretation of "lawful" is prima facie with the commander; rarely are accused mutineers acquitted, either in law or in the public mind.

The classic mutinies of maritime literature, the factual *Bounty* case and the fictional *Caine* mutiny, are timelessly compelling stories precisely because the crew members seem to have such clear justification for their actions: Bligh's unyielding discipline and Queeg's paranoid fixations. But in both stories, the ultimate sympathy of the audience is with the commander. Bligh's cruel necessity was to focus his crew on their mission in the face of the temptations of Polynesia; Queeg, until rattled by the snide arrogance of his officers, represented the faith and discipline of naval tradition against the self-congratulatory self-righteousness of his relatively "amateur" underlings, brilliant perhaps, but holding little stake in that tradition.

Effective crew, as these stories suggest, are not zombies, mindlessly following the leader. The letter of the law may say that following orders is the highest duty, but there is a still higher duty: to engage fully in the enterprise, to understand the stakes and become, in the heart at least, a stakeholder. It is of course the reciprocal obligation of effective command to so engage the crew, but a good crew member is able to make an active effort to be engaged. In naval service it was once customary for sailors to try to follow a particularly successful commander from ship to ship, not only out of loyalty or a comfort in the familiar but because followers understood the purposes and methods of the captain being followed. Whatever the skipper ordered would be done, because it had become the crew's culture to accept and follow—to be enthused about—the mission. Most extraordinary, this level of engagement would hold even in the life-and-death situations that are an accepted part of life aboard a warship and that were even more commonplace in the era of sail.

Today no leader of an undersea expedition or yachtsman with a serious offshore racing agenda would undertake a voyage without a crew whose skill, loyalty, and above all engagement with the project were not at least the equal of any ship's company in the Age of Nelson. The required expertise and the ultimate stakes may be in many ways different, but in the end the issue comes down to survival and success, in that order. Only when a proper crew is assembled can those goals be assured, or at least brought within the realm of acceptable probability.

In the end, of course, the crew lives or dies with the captain, a fact that must have been among the rueful or angry final thoughts of hundreds of thousands of mariners over the millennia. They who serve with alacrity and talent should be able to serve also with hope. It is, however, the way of the sea that ability and wisdom are not always sufficient. The brilliant Smith of the *Titanic* took hundreds of Cunard sailors—the very flower of the British merchant service—with him to their doom, with every man-jack from mate to lookout to stoker doing his duty. Ten thousand heroes have served their skippers to the last in shipwrecks that occurred unseen, unchronicled, as storms, fires, and encounters with hidden rocks and reefs snuffed out their lives, mocking their skills and all that human intelligence could accomplish. Captain and crew alike are, in the end, mortal. At some point, even the child venturing upon the sea—whether in reality or only in mind—must confront this most fundamental of realities.

WR

IX. Peril

As a species we are transfixed by tales of imminent danger and extraordinary suffering. We devour details of stories in which our fellows face situations that require surpassing courage and physical exertion and in which they have close encounters with what we can only imagine to be the pain of death. Our cultural fascination with these things transcends shallow tabloid curiosity; we are keenly aware of the millions (presumably) drowned in the biblical flood that only Noah and his family survived, and the story of Jonah, thrown into a raging sea and then swallowed alive by a great fish, sticks hard to the consciousness of Sunday school children.

For coastal peoples, storm and shipwreck have always been a fact of life. Fishing communities through the ages have experienced devastating rates of mortality, enough almost to make one wonder why anyone would follow such a dangerous line of work. Women and the young, especially, have had to deal with the deaths at sea of husbands, fathers, and other loved ones, and in low-lying communities subject to major storms, whole families have been lost in the Great Storms (often named for a year) that periodically scour the littoral. Scarcely marked by history, the sacrifice of fisherfolk has been one of great significance to the survival of our kind. A walk through a seaside cemetery is revelatory: stone after stone marked with a name, "lost at sea." In the modern world, when children's view of the food chain ends in the aisles of the supermarket, it behooves us to teach our children of the hardships our primary providers have faced, and still do. *The Perfect Storm*, after all, featured the tragic loss of a Gloucester swordfishing boat, the descendant of the codfish fleet celebrated by Kipling in *Captains Courageous*—a fact obscured if not in the book, then among the high-tech special effects in the film. The men of the *Andrea Gail* died for our luxury protein.

A century and a half ago it was also the common experience of dwellers alongshore periodically to witness the destruction of ships on the very rocks and beaches of their towns. A storm, a treacherous tide, a navigational error or minor equipment failure, and suddenly crew and passengers found themselves cast in a life-and-death drama. Where surf rescue services were available, the drama had the added feature of local men putting their own lives at risk to reach the wreck and rescue whom they could, but often enough, especially in cold weather, those on land could only watch the struggles of those aboard the disintegrating vessel, who dropped, one by one, into the frigid, turbulent sea and certain death.

Against this backdrop, lately augmented by blockbuster movies like *Titanic* and *The Perfect Storm*, watery doom has taken its place on the American cultural landscape of death. Children growing up, even in dry regions (where swimming-pool drownings are so common in some places that support groups have been gathered for parents of victims), know to regard being careful around water as essential to survival. News reports each weekend through the long, hot summer remind us that we are at risk (and that "water and alcohol don't mix," although no shoreside convenience store or brewery would support total abstinence for the operators of any boat); accidents happen, and people die.

Few young people are forced to face mortal circumstances on the water, and in reality not many do. But almost anyone who has ventured forth in a small boat has experienced the sudden tip, the unexpected wave, the near-fall that serves as a memento mori. Occurring too swiftly to generate fear in the moment, it is only on later contemplation that "what might have happened" becomes clear in the mind's eye. We resolve to be careful, more observant, next time. We add another particular danger to our internal catalogue of anxieties, but we also know that the odds are in our favor.

Those who have experienced more serious calamities on the water—a capsize, a man-overboard, a key piece of the vessel broken, a swamping, the list is endless— become more circumspect. They know the feeling of cold and fear and wetness, and the wait for rescue or the frantic efforts to put things to rights for themselves; rescue is never a certainty. It is perhaps for this reason that canoeing students are taught to swamp, right, and bail a canoe as an introductory lesson or that sailing programs spend time teaching students to cope with a capsized boat—how to work through a methodical checklist on the status of crew and vessel and then to put the boat back into operation. Operators of personal watercraft seem to undergo no such disaster training, but the "dead man" cable attached to their wrists is guaranteed to shut the vessel off in the event the operator is pitched off; it is assumed that the recovery and remounting process can be accomplished by intuition alone.

I used to sail with someone whose motto was,

"If you don't bleed, it's not a real sail." The toe-stubbings, scratchings, and slicings that seem to accompany even the briefest sail on the simplest vessel bear the motto out, and one wears the band-aid or the scab as a badge of honor: I've been sailing! By the same token, I gradually grew aware as a young sailor that the "crash boat" at the weekly youth races seldom had much direct help to offer, other than hovering near the capsized or swamped boat at a discreet distance as those aboard shouted some—not much—advice on how best to recover from the mishap. Wet and usually pretty angry, we had to put the pieces together ourselves, bail the water out, lift ourselves back aboard, bring the flapping sail and gyrating tiller under control, and put ourselves back on course. We had to solve the essential problems with our own brains and muscle, under difficult circumstances, and this was a lesson I could have learned in no other way and in no other place. Such, I have realized as an adult, is the nature of authentic experiential learning—controlled risk, problems to be solved, confident (if not always gleeful) mastery.

Serious disaster is, of course, another matter. The rapidity with which a bad situation on the water can become critical is astounding—the effects of cold water and exhaustion, perhaps exacerbating a minor injury; or else a vessel immobilized in the grip of a powerful current or wind—and those who have confronted such circumstances have learned some powerful and unsettling lessons.

In dark, stormy waters, as hope of rescue or relief seeps away, the human spirit is swiftly overwhelmed by a desire to surrender. Hypothermia intensifies despair and apathy, and so it is not so hard to understand why so many victims of accident at sea are found afloat, sometimes as if asleep, buoyed up by flotation devices that did little to keep spirits high. At first one is conscious of this strange and awful effect, and in the best of circumstances (or in the worst, for a few individuals with astounding powers of emotional resilience) it is recognized for what it is and conquered by positive thought. But once it has introduced itself, like an unattractive seatmate on a long journey, its presence is always felt, the possibility of a lengthy and final conversation astir in the back of the mind. Survivors have written of this, and others know it but do not wish to tell. Like a patient "fighting" cancer, the victim in immediate peril at sea is expected to call upon the rich reserves of physical fortitude and moral courage we have read about in adventure stories; the realization that these qualities are limited, or that some situations are indeed inescapably fatal, is somehow shameful. If we are to die at sea, we must do so in heroic struggle—or we must die in embarrassment.

Yet somehow we must learn to hope. In a strange way, governments have become purveyors of that hope through the process of regulating and marking dangers on the waters. One of the young American republic's first acts in the closing years of the eighteenth century had been to develop a system of aids to navigation, including lighthouses and, in time, standardized charts produced by government agencies. Even so, accidents happened, and with ship-to-ship and ship-to-shore communication iffy until World War I, the scale of maritime disasters rose, not declined. With immigrant ships packed to the gunwales with paying customers and all overseas commerce and most coastal trade moving by water, the crowded sea and riverways became death zones. Accounts of steamship explosions and fires, collisions, ships reported as overdue and never heard from again, and seemingly random groundings and sinkings filled the pages of newspapers from coast to coast; reporters worked overtime to find adjectives to describe the carnage. Survival tales were often as lurid (and as popular) as stories of mass death, with frostbite, exposure, and burns among the more terrible ordeals that victims might experience. Circulation offices thrived on the imperilment and death of those upon the sea.

We sometimes believe that in other times or other cultures, where death seems more common, people are hardened to the experience. Sociologists tell us that this is seldom the case, that sorrow and compassion do not arise in inverse proportion to need. As young people read the history of maritime disaster and of war at sea, let them never succumb to the notion that "so many people were dying, it didn't matter that much." For proof of this contention, along with those memorial stones to the lost in seaside graveyards, look at the personal nature of historical efforts to promote the safety of life at sea.

Lighthouses, those beautiful, distinctive, and now historic structures that were also technical marvels in their time, were once operated by a workforce notable for its ability to do absolutely dependable service under conditions that were simply horrific. Isolated, facing extremes of wind and weather, and charged with maintaining the light (and audible signals in fog) every day, regardless of any impediment, lighthouse keepers and their families were among the popular heroes of the 1800s, and tales of their extraordinary courage and devotion to keeping their lanterns lit were also standard newspaper fare. It was in this era that the lighthouse, the beacon, became so utterly associated with the idea of hope; along with warning the mariner away from danger, a steadily flashing beam of light was also a sign of safe haven as universally understood by those at sea as a motel billboard is to motorists today.

This hopefulness has no doubt contributed to the romance associated with lighthouses. By definition situated in stunning, picturesque locations, lighthouses—even the cast-iron pipe structures common in Southern waters—have today a cult following. Serious enthusiasts travel from light to light, taking photographs and gathering memories, and they can acquire miniature models of virtually every lighthouse on the continent from stores that specialize in lighthouse books, paintings, calendars, models, memorabilia, and other trinkets. It is not difficult to empathize with lighthouse buffs, for there is a singular beauty to the buildings and a compelling story in their history and purpose. And they all have great views.

Beachgoers in certain coastal towns may note rowboats drawn up next to lifeguard chairs. They may even see the guards out for a row, and it is not hard to understand the rationale of having these little vessels available along the immediate shore. What visitors may not know, however, is that the lifeguards' boats are the modern incarnation of one of the most rugged and dangerous enterprises ever sponsored by the United States government, the U.S. Lifesaving Service. In the mid-1800s, shipwrecks along the coast had become so common, and their costs so devastating, that the government decided to consolidate and expand the various lifeboat rescue services that had developed randomly in particularly dangerous locations. With standardized (though regionally built) rowing vessels and standard procedures, led by professionals and manned by locally recruited paid volunteers, the lifeboat crew stood ready, with its members regularly walking the shore and ready to spring into action, to bring to an end the tragic—some also thought disgraceful—phenomenon of beachside shipwrecks resulting in loss of life. Human-powered in its methods and impossibly dangerous, the Lifesaving Service worked; its remnants survive on American beaches today in the lifeguards' rowboats and abroad in the still-strong traditions of the lifesaving teams of the Channel Islands and other remote and treacherous locales.

Today's rescuers, readers of *The Perfect Storm* will recollect, arrive at the scene by motor lifeboat, by airplane, and by helicopter. Nearly as dangerous as ever, in part because technology enables rescues to be made in locations and under conditions that would have made even the attempt inconceivable in years past, the Lifesaving Service—part of the Coast Guard in the United States and Canada—seems never to lack for volunteers, a testament to the depth of the human desire to serve and save others as well as a tribute to the great record and high standards set by rescuers themselves. Let the young person who is obsessed with the sea and who is not cowed by the most rigorous of life's tests consider this profession, at least for a while.

Of course, in the end there will be terrible images. A curious aspect of humankind's curiosity about the nature of dying is our exuberance in singing about it. Homer does not shrink from descriptions of the drownings of Odysseus' crew members any more than he is reticent to offer the inside view of "black death swirling down" behind the eyes of victims sliced and skewered in battle. Children shout happily how "Sad, so sad" it was that the mighty *Titanic* went down and "all the husbands, and wives, little children [like the singers themselves] lost their lives." Not just albums but shelves of boxed sets could be made of recorded shipwreck songs. Some are lugubrious, others tediously factual, but many are in fact cheery, and almost all have been written by mariners and shore-dwellers— and many composed at sea, perhaps in the teeth of a gale. To sing of a circumstance worse than one's own may help keep courage, and perspective—and maybe even the singer—alive. Some songs focus on individual heroics, but most just tell the story, down to the bitter end.

Calamity at sea has played a smaller role in the fine arts than in popular forms. Longfellow's mawkish *Wreck of the Hesperus* may have evoked drawing-room tears from nineteenth-century maidens who visualized themselves as the loving daughter meeting a ghastly fate on the reef of Norman's Woe (a real place, off Cape Ann, Massachusetts), but great shipwreck poetry is hard to find. One thinks of Géricault's *Raft of the Medusa* and Winslow Homer's *The Gulf Stream* as iconic images of death at sea, but what gives these paintings moral force is their implication of the dreadful fate that awaits the obviously blameless victims. Even John Singleton Copley's *Watson and the Shark* is relatively tame, a diverting multicultural tableau softened, in part, by our knowledge that the skinny-dipping Brook Watson, clearly a risk-taker, in time parlayed his adventurous spirit and good fortune into the lord mayoralty of London. Other paintings of shipwrecks and maritime disaster are remarkable for their conventional sameness, their technical emphasis on form and light rather than on human extremity.

How do we contemplate, yet alone face, this extremity? In our fascination with the action of death at sea, even the most exacting chroniclers tend to shy away from representing, or even interpreting, the moment when the light of humanity is extinguished and empty death is triumphant; only the boldest, or coldest, of authors ventures close to this extremity. The vastness of the sea and its unseen depths ultimately frightens us even as it draws us.

WR

X. ABYSS

In one of the earlier *Pickwick Papers*, Dickens's main character is approached by a man while standing on a bridge on a fine summer's day. "Did it ever strike you, on such a morning as this, that drowning would be happiness and peace?" asks the man, as Pickwick recoils. "The calm, cool water seems to me to murmur an invitation to repose and rest. A bound, a splash, a brief struggle; there is an eddy for an instant, it gradually subsides into a gentle ripple; the waters have closed above your head, and the world has closed upon your miseries and misfortunes forever," the man continues, and shortly walks away. The genial Pickwick, the placid realist, is left gaping.

The contemplation of death by water has at once terrified and enticed humans for ages. Like the eyes of a weaving snake, unfathomable depths hold for humans a timeless, often morbid, fascination. As a literary trope, suicide by drowning is the chosen mode of some of fiction's most self-reflective characters, from Faulkner's Quentin Compson in *The Sound and the Fury* to Kate Chopin's Edna Pontellier in *The Awakening*—not to mention of course Narcissus himself, the archetype of destructive self-reflection. The power of the deep is its very capacity for resisting penetration, for throwing back at us the very image we project; that the reflected image is often distorted only adds to the fatal mystery. How seldom we recognize our own delusions!

The child gazing hard at the water as it slides by the hull of a vessel or passes under a bridge will be drawn into the mystery. He or she may invent games and fantasies—Pooh-sticks and little mermaids—to project meaning into the depths, and when on occasion what is below reveals itself in the shiny swirl of a fish or the sudden glimpse of a rock projecting upward from the bottom, the mind and heart quicken with interest. Will there be more, will these things manifest themselves again? Is there danger? Is there a kind of treasure?

What does Jim Hawkins think about as he watches the sea roll by and listens to the sly prattle of Long John ever drawing him more deeply into complicity with his nefarious schemes? What pulls Conrad's Marlowe, a companionable, sophisticated man, ever to the water, from the sea of his youth to the Congo River, even as his fellows "swallow the anchor" to become men of affairs? The enduring popularity and impact of literature in which such characters test themselves and explore the meaning of their own humanity on the sea gives clear evidence of the primal connection between our species and the sea.

In literature, the depths of the sea and not merely its reflective surface prove themselves an awesome force. The intensity of Jules Verne's Nemo, even beyond James Mason's portrayal in the Disney film, is focused on visiting justice on the unjust—through acts of violence committed during a journey of 20,000 leagues under the sea; Nemo is nothing if not one of literature's early terrorists, casting aside conventional morality in the name of a higher good that only he and his band of fanatical followers—suicide bombers, in the end—can understand enough to embrace.

And Melville gives us a whole shipload of moral question marks whose character and fate are revealed in the crucible of the sea through the catalyst of the White Whale—itself an empty cartoon balloon into which each of the *Pequod's* crew members, from Ahab to Starbuck to Fedallah to Queequeg to Ishmael, can insert his own sermonette on Last Things. To embark upon the sea with Ahab is truly to be swallowed by the moral abyss, and Melville only saves Ishmael in order to have a plausible voice through which to tell the tale.

For the curious mind that fancies being pulled below the surface of the water but eschews fiction, there are the explorations of *The Undersea World of Jacques Cousteau* and his successors. For a time a half century ago, the best minds in oceanography sought to descend into the true abyss, those gouges in the floor of the ocean that approach seven miles in depth, a full seventh farther below sea level than Mount Everest lies above it. When at last the Piccards' bathyscaphe *Trieste* hit bottom in the Marianas Trench off the Philippines in 1960, humankind had sent one of its own into one of the most terrible environments in the solar system, where crushing pressure, inexorable cold, and impenetrable darkness give less on which to look or focus inquiry than even the dusty surface of the Moon, first visited only a few years later. And like the Moon, the far depths of the ocean have been visited rarely since; the explorations of underwater thermal vents and their animal and mineral products take place at a relatively congenial depth of only a mile or so, a mere fraction of the way "down."

What lies below the layers humans can reach with relative ease (in truth, only a couple of hundred feet for scuba divers, a bit more for tethered divers in full-pressure suits, and just a few thousand feet for all but the most sophisticated manned submersibles) remains one of our planet's most intriguing mysteries. In earlier chapters I made reference to deep-ocean fish, but in fact we know little about their kind, their numbers, and their habits. We have yet to land a living giant squid of full size, and a number of species are known by only a single specimen; some are known only by a handful of sightings. How evolution has dealt with deep-ocean vertebrates and other undiscovered life-forms will perhaps come clear as incentives for profit encourage more exploration, either for energy sources or for valuable minerals.

Here the future may hold untold wonders for the young person seeking to build a life upon a fascination with the sea. Oceanography, marine geology, marine biology, and the development of technologies that will further our understanding of the waters, how they move, and what lives in them are undergoing a knowledge explosion as you read this, and the field will beckon harder still as we begin to come to grips with the role of the sea and the hidden complexities of the hydrologic cycle in global warming. Then, too, ocean currents and tides may yet be harnessed in a way that will enable us to abandon our dependency on fossil fuels—although these, too, may lie in untold profusion below the sea.

The sea giveth, and the sea taketh away. The power of the waters of the Earth both to provide and to destroy is a continuum; like all things on Earth, there is a season, a cycle, to every aspect of the sea's behavior. As a species homo sapiens has been remarkably adept at harnessing the potential of the sea—by traveling upon it, by reaping its bounties, by finding spiritual strength in its generative potency and its sheer magnitude. We have also been remarkably maladroit in how we treat it, polluting and wasting resources even as we continue to develop new ways to harm and kill ourselves on it, by accident or by acts of war. We act as if we own the sea, and in return the sea, like a dog shaking off an ill-fitting collar, reminds us that we do not, we cannot.

Our artists and poets have found and will continue to find in the sea the inspiration for works that explore our relationship to nature, to one another, to our gods, and to our innermost selves. The true artist contemplates the abyss, unlike Pickwick's companion, not as a way out of the human condition but rather as the setting for an exploration of the most profound depths of what it means to be human.

AUTHOR

Peter Gow was born and raised among educators and grew up near Lake Erie. As he grew older, he ventured eastward during the summers to the bays of eastern Long Island and, after graduating from Yale University and earning his master's at Brown, he settled in eastern New England. He has been a teacher of English and history in independent schools for thirty years, currently at Beaver Country Day School. He has also worked at Girl Scout sailing camps on Martha's Vineyard, Cape Cod, and in New York's Adirondack Mountains.

Peter has been writing on maritime, historical, and educational topics since his debut as a contributor to the sailing magazine parody, *Yaahting* (he wrote the legendary "How to Walk Down a Dock"). He is a regular contributor to *Independent School* magazine, and his most recent book is on teacher recruiting and training. He lives with his family—spouse, children, and cats—in Dedham, Massachusetts, where his daily commute offers vistas of the Charles River flowing past strip malls and fast-food joints.

ACKNOWLEDGMENTS

Elsewhere I have spoken in dedicatory terms of those who have inspired the sentiment and spirit of this book, but there are a handful of others whose support for and interest in this project have been of elemental value.

My good friends and educational all-stars Sarah Jencks, Kate Silver Rabinow, Ellen Winn, and Rebecca Yacono all read the earliest draft of the manuscript with their usual clear-eyed intelligence; my colleague Tim Parson, a devotee of the Maine coast, also gave it a thoughtful look. The bemused response of all these early readers led me to make what I hope are major improvements in the text.

Above all, the people at WoodenBoat Publications have both humbled me and earned my undying devotion, editor Jane Crosen for her gentle hand and Scot Bell for his energetic, sensitive, and graceful approach to turning an eccentric little essay into a beautiful and readable book.

THE WATERY REALM

The Watery Realm is a romantic's contemplation of the ways in which bodies of water—lakes, rivers, and seas—inspire the human spirit and ignite curiosity and yearning in those who venture onto, into, or near them. Looking at water through the lenses of geography, language, natural history, and multiple aspects of the human experience of water, readers are carried deep into their own primal connection with water and the watery realm.

Rather than being the last word on the subject, *The Watery Realm* is intended to initiate an active and pleasurable response in the reader and to inspire reminiscence, reflection, speculation, idyll, and fantasy. Boat fanatics, beach bums, sailors, naturalists, linguists, surfers, and readers of maritime lore and literature will all be reminded of the infinite joys and possibilities of the watery realm—the world of sea and shore, tall ship and kayak, lake and stream, shell and shark.

Published by WoodenBoat Books
Naskeag Road, PO Box 78
Brooklin, Maine 04616 USA
www.woodenboat.com

ISBN-13: 978-0-937822-91-3
ISBN-10: 0-937822-91-4

9 780937 822913

$17.95